SOCIAL MOVEMENTS IN AMERICA

BY DUCHESS HARRIS, JD, PHD

WITH MARTHA LUNDIN

CONTENT CONSULTANT

HEATH FOGG DAVIS, PHD
DIRECTOR, GENDER, SEXUALITY,
AND WOMEN'S STUDIES PROGRAM
TEMPLE UNIVERSITY

Essential Library

An Imprint of Abdo Publishing | abdobooks.com

ABDOBOOKS.COM

Published by Abdo Publishing, a division of ABDO, PO Box 398166, Minneapolis, Minnesota 55439. Copyright © 2020 by Abdo Consulting Group, Inc. International copyrights reserved in all countries. No part of this book may be reproduced in any form without written permission from the publisher. Essential Library™ is a trademark and logo of Abdo Publishing.

Printed in the United States of America, North Mankato, Minnesota.
022019
092019

THIS BOOK CONTAINS
RECYCLED MATERIALS

Cover Photos: Shutterstock Images (hand), (sign), (gender symbols)
Interior Photos: NY Daily News Archive/New York Daily News/Getty Images, 5; Juan Camilo Bernal/Shutterstock Images, 7; Glynnis Jones/Shutterstock Images, 11; Richard Corkery/NY Daily News/Getty Images, 14–15; Nicolas McComber/ iStockphoto, 18; McCarthy/Daily Express/Hulton Archive/Getty Images, 22; Mariette Pathy Allen/Reportage Archive/Getty Images, 24; Jon Carroll/Shutterstock Images, 27; Paul Sakuma/AP Images, 31; Mark Wilson/AP Images, 33; Shutterstock Images, 37, 91; Kathy Hutchins/Shutterstock Images, 40; Fox Network/Photofest, 43; Mary Altaffer/AP Images, 44; Aaron Amat/Shutterstock Images, 46; Leonard Zhukovsky, 49; J. Scott Applewhite/AP Images, 51; MedicalRF/Science Source, 53; Sara Krulwich/ New York Times Co./Archive Photos/Getty Images, 55; Monkey Business Images/ Shutterstock Images, 56; Kobby Dagan/Shutterstock Images, 61; iStockphoto, 63; Joe Raedle/Getty Images News/Getty Images, 64; Kristi Blokhin/Shutterstock Images, 71; Jacquelyn Martin/AP Images, 73; Syda Productions/Shutterstock Images, 75; Focus Features/Photofest, 78; Gustavo Frazao/Shutterstock Images, 80–81; AJR Photo/Shutterstock Images, 83; Beatriz Vera/Shutterstock Images, 84; Cartoon Network/Photofest, 92; Erik McGregor/Pacific Press/LightRocket/Getty Images, 96

Editor: Megan Ellis
Series Designer: Melissa Martin

LIBRARY OF CONGRESS CONTROL NUMBER: 2018965969

PUBLISHER'S CATALOGING-IN-PUBLICATION DATA

Names: Harris, Duchess, author. | Lundin, Martha, author.
Title: LGBTQ social movements in America / by Duchess Harris and Martha Lundin.
Description: Minneapolis, Minnesota : Abdo Publishing, 2020 | Series: Being LGBTQ in America | Includes online resources and index.
Identifiers: ISBN 9781532119088 (lib. bdg.) | ISBN 9781532173264 (ebook)
Subjects: LCSH: LGBTQ people--Juvenile literature. | Social movements--United States--History--20th century--Juvenile literature. | Sexual minority community--Juvenile literature. | Minorities--Civil rights--United States-- Juvenile literature.
Classification: DDC 323.3--dc23

CONTENTS

THE STONEWALL
RIOTS

The Stonewall Inn on Christopher Street in Greenwich Village, New York City, was busy in the early morning hours of June 28, 1969. People in the lesbian, gay, bisexual, transgender, and queer (LGBTQ) community gathered at the dark bar to dance and find others like themselves.

Around 1:20 in the morning, a group of a dozen police officers entered the Stonewall Inn. They shut down the bar and began arresting patrons for kissing, underage drinking, and not wearing enough "gender-appropriate" clothing.[1] The police officers took the people outside, where a police van waited for them. Some of the bar patrons resisted being loaded into the vehicle. One officer hit a woman on the head with his nightstick. She called out to the crowd gathered outside the bar, "Why don't you guys do something?"[2]

Suddenly, people in the crowd began throwing things at the police. At first they were small things such as coins, but

they soon turned into bottles and other debris. After years of police abuse, the drag queens and trans people were done cooperating. A lesbian who dressed in a butch, or masculine, way reportedly escaped the police van and began rocking the vehicle.

Drag queens, or men who dress up as and perform on stage as women, and transgender (trans) people, or people whose gender identity does not match the sex they were assigned at birth, led the charge against the police force. The police quickly lost control of the crowd. The officers locked themselves inside the Stonewall Inn, away from the angry protesters. A tactical squad was dispatched to calm the riot outside, but there was little anyone could do. Protesters tried to break down the door of the Stonewall Inn with a parking meter.

LANGUAGE, LABELS, AND FLUIDITY

Labels in the 1900s were much different, and much more limited, than they are in 2018. Transgender people were often called *transsexuals* or *transvestites*. These labels were created by the medical community. Many trans people used these labels for themselves as well. Others chose, and continue to choose, to call themselves *gay*. *Gay* was often used as an umbrella term for the LGBTQ community. It described a sexuality or gender that was outside the social norms of heterosexuality and strict gender roles. Today, words such as *transvestite* are not used unless a person specifically requests to be called that term. As of 2019, *transgender* or *trans* were often used as broad descriptions of people who are not cisgender. This book uses era-appropriate labels wherever possible. However, it is important to remember that labels and identities are always shifting.

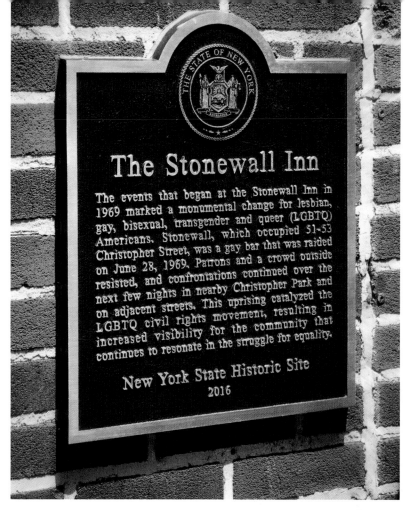

The Stonewall Inn was designated as a historic site in 2016.

Some people threw homemade bombs known as Molotov cocktails, which caused fires.

Many people assumed the protest would end that night, but there was continued violence outside the Stonewall Inn for the next six days. It is estimated that more than 1,000 people joined in what are now known as the Stonewall riots.[3] After the riots, LGBTQ people held meetings and formed new groups, intent on making social change. They organized a memorial march. Many activists today label Stonewall as the beginning of the modern LGBTQ rights movement.

A CORRUPT SYSTEM

Many New York laws made it hard or even impossible for LGBTQ people to live openly in the 1960s. For example, one law prohibited bars that served LGBTQ people from receiving liquor licenses, which were necessary to sell alcohol legally. Lawmakers justified this law by stating that a group of LGBTQ people drinking was "disorderly."[4] To get around this law, many gay bars were owned by members of the Mafia. The Mafia was an organized collection of criminals who operated in New York. Members of various Mafia groups bribed New York police to ignore the illegal acts happening in the bars. LGBTQ people found a place where they could gather free from harassment. Police officers still made frequent raids on the bars to maintain the appearance of order or to receive bigger payoffs from the Mafia.

WHY STONEWALL?

Greenwich Village was and is filled with artists and musicians. It tends to be more accepting of LGBTQ people than other parts of New York. However, the Stonewall Inn was not well regarded by much of the LGBTQ community in New York. It was dark and dirty, and the crowd that gathered at the Stonewall Inn was

NOT JUST STONEWALL

Three years before the uprising at the Stonewall Inn, drag queens and trans women in San Francisco, California, fought back against police harassment at Compton's. Compton's was a 24-hour eatery. Employees at Compton's often called the police to clear out the drag queens and trans women who frequented the restaurant. Amanda St. Jaymes was a trans woman who owned a hotel near Compton's. She said that one night, trans women "just got tired of it. We got tired of being harassed. We got tired of being made to go into the men's room when we were dressed like women. We wanted our rights."[5]

That night, women at Compton's threw sugar shakers and silverware at the police. A crowd outside wrecked one of the cop cars and set a newsstand on fire. Despite the commotion, the event wasn't reported in the news. Even the people involved at Compton's didn't talk about it much. The only surviving report came out in 1972. Tamara Ching, an Asian American trans woman, said that none of the women thought this protest was important. She said, "We lived to survive day to day. We didn't realize we'd made history."[6]

looked down on by some people in the LGBTQ community. That was because the Stonewall Inn was one of the few places where drag queens, trans people, and LGBTQ youth experiencing homelessness were accepted.

Stonewall was also a prime target for police raids because of its large population of drag queens and trans people. New York had anti-sodomy laws that made sex acts between two people of the same sex illegal, but these laws were difficult to enforce. However, New York had what was called the Three Articles rule. People were required to be wearing at least three articles of clothing that corresponded to their sex assigned at birth.[7] The cross-dressing violations were easy to prove. For trans people, that became a significant issue.

Raids at LGBTQ bars across the city were common, but they were especially common in Greenwich Village. Greenwich Village had a large population of trans women and sex workers, and many went to the Stonewall Inn after work every night. The bar was important because it was one of the few places where LGBTQ people who also belonged to other minority groups were able to build their own community. Most other bars were predominantly white. They were not always welcoming to trans people and people of color (POC).

Today, Stonewall is recognized as the beginning of the LGBTQ rights movement, but sometimes it goes unrecognized that

THE WHITEWASHING OF STONEWALL

Miss Major was one of the trans women at the Stonewall riots. In an interview, Major, a black trans activist, talked about how white, cisgender gay men are often portrayed as the leaders of the uprising. A statue was erected outside the Stonewall Inn in 1992 to commemorate the uprising. In describing the statue, Major said it looked like it was "made from flour and sugar!"[8]

It's not only statues that are whitewashed. Even films leave out transgender and POC participants in the Stonewall riots. The 2015 movie *Stonewall* cast a white male lead. Many trans activists thought this choice rewrote history in a hurtful way. Miss Major said,

> [White people] were not the ones getting slugged or having stones thrown at them. It's just aggravating. And hurtful! For all the girls who are no longer here who can't say anything, this movie just acts like they didn't exist.[9]

LGBTQ marches during Pride in New York City pass by the Stonewall Inn.

drag queens and trans women of color were the first to fight back. In the wake of the uprising, trans voices were drowned out by their cisgender (cis) peers. Cisgender people have gender identities that match the sex they were assigned at birth. On the anniversary of the Stonewall riots in 1973, transgender activist Sylvia Rivera was booed by cisgender activists when she discussed the struggles of trans people. Rivera famously yelled, "Y'all better quiet down!" to encourage others in the community to listen.[10] She continued to speak over the booing crowd. Eventually they listened to her story of the violence that affected trans people. By the end of the speech, the crowd chanted with her.

SOCIAL MOVEMENTS

Social movements are defined by a collection of people working toward a social goal. The LGBTQ community is made up of many different people with a variety of beliefs. LGBTQ equality is the overall goal of the social movement. But equality has many facets. Smaller movements occur within the community. They may work to create a fairer and more just society for LGBTQ Americans. Some of these movements focus on employment equality. Others focus on fair treatment in the medical community. Some movement proponents believe violence is the most effective course of action. But others think LGBTQ people should work within the system to create change.

The Stonewall Inn remains an icon of LGBTQ equality because it set the stage for social movement groups in the

STONEWALL'S LEGACY

In 2000, the Stonewall Inn was listed on the register of historic locations. In 2016, two days before New York's Pride March, President Barack Obama made a historic decision. Obama designated the Stonewall Inn as the country's first national monument dedicated to LGBTQ rights. In his statement, Obama said:

> I believe our national parks should reflect the full story of our country—the richness and diversity and uniquely American spirit that has always defined us, that we are stronger together. That out of many, we are one.[11]

Today, Stonewall is still a bar that people can visit. When same-sex marriage was legalized in 2015, many people gathered outside Stonewall to celebrate and dance.

years to come. However, LGBTQ people have been organizing, resisting, and socially gathering in the United States for hundreds of years. The LGBTQ rights movement that people recognize today relies on grassroots organizations. These groups create political change not only in smaller communities but also at the state and national levels. Social movements are fluid organizations. They shift and change membership as times and needs change. In the course of the 1900s and 2000s, social movements have helped LGBTQ people gain civil rights at the local, state, and federal levels.

DISCUSSION STARTERS

- What would you have done if you were at the Stonewall Inn the night of the police raid? Explain your answer.

- Can you think of other social movements that are around today? How do they make a difference at the local and national levels?

- What is something you think needs to change in society? What do you think is the first step toward making that change?

After the uprising at Stonewall, LGBTQ rights activists organized marches and other events.

BEFORE AND AFTER
STONEWALL

LGBTQ social movement groups existed before the Stonewall riots. Groups sprung up in the early 1900s out of a need for community. At first these groups were strictly social. But as the groups grew, and as attitudes in the country changed, groups also changed their focus. Eventually they saw how, together, they could create meaningful change in the LGBTQ community.

BEFORE

Henry Gerber, a German immigrant, lived in Chicago, Illinois, with his family. He enlisted in the US Army at the end of World War I (1914–1918). While stationed in Germany, he was exposed to a growing and vibrant movement of gays and lesbians. The Scientific-Humanitarian Committee in Berlin, Germany, was interested in promoting a wider acceptance of LGBTQ

THE "SOCIAL" ASPECT OF SOCIAL MOVEMENTS

Prior to the 1950s, LGBTQ people were isolated from each other. Fears about homosexuality spread into work and community life. Social movements were important for LGBTQ people. Groups in these movements allowed LGBTQ people to talk about their lives openly for the first time. Furthermore, they were met not by questions but by nodding heads and empathy. Communities of support allowed LGBTQ people to create political and social change.

people in Germany. One of the founders, Magnus Hirschfield, also founded the Institute for Sexual Science. These organizations were decades ahead of those in other nations when it came to research on sexuality. As a result, gay and lesbian people in Germany were more accepted than in other parts of the world.[1] When Gerber returned to the United States in 1923, he wanted to do something similar.

In 1924, Gerber founded the Society for Human Rights. The end of World War I brought with it an expanding LGBTQ population in Chicago. Immigrants from around the world, particularly German immigrants, settled in Chicago. Many people found freedom from familial and religious obligations in the midwestern United States. Harassment remained a problem in Chicago, though. There were anti-cross-dressing laws, and public acceptance of gender and sexual variance from societal norms was limited. Gerber hoped to change that with his organization. However, many people were afraid of going public. It took Gerber several months to find six other people to join his group. He began publishing a newsletter, *Friendship and Freedom*, which promoted the acceptance of homosexuality.

In 1925, police raided Gerber's home and arrested him. His writings were confiscated, and he was held in jail for three days. Though the Society for Human Rights did not last long, it was an important step in the United States' journey toward LGBTQ equality.

The United States didn't have another large LGBTQ rights organization until the 1950s. In 1948, Harry Hay called for a gay rights movement. Hay and seven other men formed the Mattachine Foundation in Los Angeles, California, in the winter of 1950. The foundation had roots in communism,

THE DEFINITION OF GAY

The word *gay* did not always mean someone who is attracted to people of the same sex. It also describes something happy or joyful. According to the PBS Digital Studios show *Origin of Everything*, LGBTQ people began using the term *gay* in the mid-1900s. Previously, the accepted term was *homosexual*, though this term was created by doctors who wanted to cure same-sex attraction.

Instead of *homosexual*, LGBTQ people began to use the term *gay* as a code word that other people in the community would understand but would fly under the radar of people outside the community. According to professor George Chauncey, "A lesbian could say she met a gay gal the night before and her lesbian friend would know exactly what she meant while her straight boss would have no idea what she was talking about."[2]

Many LGBTQ people in the United States gathered in San Francisco, California. Castro Street is an area of the city where many LGBTQ people live and work.

which was a political stance that became dangerous to hold in the United States during the Cold War (1947–1991). Still, the men knew there was value in being able to meet together. The Mattachine Foundation grew quickly, spreading out across Los Angeles and into San Francisco and eventually to New York.

In the first three years, the foundation had monthly discussion groups. These discussion groups were important not only for creating a community but also for raising awareness in the surrounding neighborhoods and cities. As member Dorr Legg recalled, "There were tens of thousands of people in the L.A. area involved with it. . . . You could go to a Mattachine meeting every night of every week."[3]

By 1953, people felt tension from the federal investigations of suspected communists. The founders were afraid that if they were exposed, their group could be jeopardized. They stepped down from their leadership roles. The Mattachine Foundation became the Mattachine Society and adopted a new mission statement. In its new statement, the society shied away from radicalism. It argued that gay and lesbian people should try to blend in with the rest of society. Its work continued through 1969. An offshoot of the group, ONE Inc., published the first pro-LGBTQ magazine in the United States. It was called *ONE Magazine*.

In San Francisco, a group of women came together in 1955 to form the Daughters of Bilitis. It began as a secret social gathering and organization of lesbians. This social aspect was particularly important

WHAT'S IN A NAME?

Because of a lack of community support, LGBTQ social groups needed code names to keep members safe. The Mattachine Foundation was named after a group of medieval travelers. These men traveled from village to village sharing music and ballads. Within these performances were messages of social justice. The Daughters of Bilitis named itself after a collection of poems. The poems focused on Bilitis, a woman who was romantically involved with the female Greek poet Sappho. These names weren't immediately recognizable to people outside the LGBTQ community. The careful name choices allowed gay and lesbian people to be social without being ostracized.

ONE MAGAZINE

In 1953, a group of volunteer editors and writers began producing a new magazine out of a small office in Los Angeles, California. The magazine, *ONE*, was one of the few magazines to focus on LGBTQ rights issues in the mid-1900s. The first issues of *ONE* were sold in bars, but the magazine soon expanded to a mailing list. At the time of its publication, being LGBTQ was illegal in every state, and the federal government was harassing and firing LGBTQ employees. The US Postal Service refused to deliver the magazine, calling it "obscene."[4] The company took the post office to court. Initially, the court said the post office was allowed to refuse service. But *ONE* appealed the lower court's decision. The case reached the Supreme Court in 1957. The court ruled in favor of *ONE*. The opinion of the court was a single sentence: "Speech in favor of homosexuality is not inherently obscene."[5] The 2,000 readers of the magazine were able to receive it in the mail.[6] The Supreme Court's decision allowed LGBTQ media to flourish.

for lesbians in the 1950s because of the rigid gender roles expected of women. Soon, chapters of the Daughters of Bilitis sprang up around the country. As the organization expanded, so did the mission of the group. What began as a social group became increasingly political. It began working with the Mattachine Society. The groups held public forums to educate the public. The Daughters of Bilitis worked to create a broader understanding of homosexuality in San Francisco. In October 1956, the group began publishing the first lesbian periodical, *The Ladder*.

AFTER

Before Stonewall, many social movements and LGBTQ groups wanted to be seen as respectable. They were careful with their image in the larger society. They hoped respectability would gain societal approval. After the Stonewall riots, some people believed a change was necessary. They advocated taking a more radical approach, resorting to violence if necessary. Groups could not agree about the best way to gain equality. The Mattachine Society and the Daughters of Bilitis were unable to keep up with the increasing militancy, or use of violent tactics, of social groups.

Immediately after the Stonewall riots, a group of LGBTQ activists formed the Gay Liberation Front (GLF). Many of these activists were young and part of the growing counterculture—a group of people going against the norm—in New York. They recognized that the methods of the Mattachine Society and the Daughters of Bilitis did not change public opinion of LGBTQ people. Wanting better treatment

THE LADDER AND ASSIMILATION

The Ladder was revolutionary for giving voice to lesbian experiences. Up until that point in history, the LGBTQ rights movement was centered on cisgender gay men. However, The Ladder and the Daughters of Bilitis were not without their own flaws. They have been criticized for focusing on white, affluent women, while leaving out women of color and women without economic means. The Daughters of Bilitis also argued that lesbians weren't any different than straight women. Because of this, The Ladder often frowned on women dressing in masculine clothing. The magazine recommended traditional feminine dress. By the early 1970s, fighting within the group over leadership and the path the group should take caused the national chapter of the Daughters of Bilitis to disband.

from their government and neighbors, the GLF had a radical mission statement. It supported militant civil rights groups in the early 1970s and continued to take a direct action approach to its political and social activism. Direct action entails public protests, strikes, and demonstrations to create change as well as to educate.

Many people agreed with this stance, but others weren't convinced—even some members of the organization itself. In December 1969, a small group of members from the

The GLF marched in support of other causes in the 1970s. These included women's rights and rights for African Americans.

GLF—Jim Owles, Marty Robinson, Arthur Evans, Arthur Bell, and Kay Tobin Lahusen—split off to form the Gay Activists Alliance (GAA). The GAA did not agree with the GLF's decision to support other activist organizations. The new group thought it was more important to focus only on gay and lesbian issues.

The GAA was significantly less militant than the GLF. The members preferred to use zaps, which were public confrontations with political figures. Zaps were designed to draw a lot of media attention to the group and to the target's homophobic attitudes. These actions ranged from throwing a pie in a politician's face to running across a TV news station set with a banner.

Their group began to grow. With it, a desire for more social opportunities rose. In 1971, the GAA began renting an old firehouse in New York. It became a center for social gatherings, with a weekly dance held in the building. However, within the next two years, the organization would dissolve due to disagreements and members splitting off to form separate organizations.

It was easy for the media and politicians to forget about trans women of color and homeless youth. The faces of most LGBTQ rights groups were white, gay, cisgender men. These people had a lot more privilege than the trans population. They also used their appearance to their advantage. White, cisgender,

Sylvia Rivera organized safe spaces for trans teens in New York City.

gay men looked like the heterosexual majority. Trans women of color did not. Racism and transphobia worked in favor of the gay organizations. Groups were often so focused on any change that they didn't think about who was being ignored.

Trans women Marsha P. Johnson and Sylvia Rivera recognized that organizations such as the GAA and the GLF ignored the needs of trans people and LGBTQ youth. Johnson and Rivera started Street Transvestites Action Revolutionaries (STAR) in 1969. They rented the upper floor of a house in Greenwich Village as a space for homeless youth and trans sex workers. According to Rivera, "We were trying to get away from the Mafia's control at the bars."[7] The new STAR house allowed these people greater security in a safe environment. Many people recognize Rivera and Johnson as leaders in the LGBTQ rights movements for their commitment to inclusivity and mutual support for community members.

DISCUSSION STARTERS

- How would the LGBTQ rights movement be different without groups such as Mattachine and the Daughters of Bilitis? Do you think LGBTQ people would have the same rights they do now?

- Marsha P. Johnson and Sylvia Rivera are often erased in LGBTQ history. Knowing how important they are, why do you think history books leave them out?

- Social change can be enacted in many ways. What do you think is most effective and why?

3

MARCHES AND
PRIDE PARADES

As the one-year anniversary of the Stonewall riots approached, LGBTQ advocates in New York knew they wanted to commemorate the event. People gathered on June 28, 1970, in front of the Stonewall Inn. A few hundred people began marching up Sixth Avenue to Central Park.[1] They called the event the Christopher Street Liberation Day March. As they marched, holding posters demanding equality, other LGBTQ people joined in. By the time the crowd reached Central Park, more than 2,000 people had gathered together.[2] As news of Christopher Street spread, a sister march was held in Los Angeles. Marches in solidarity were held all over the country and eventually throughout the world.

Today, Pride is known as a celebration of LGBTQ people and their allies. It is something filled with rainbow flags and a parade. But that first march didn't have parade floats or music. The rainbow flag hadn't been created yet. The first march was

a protest. The Christopher Street Liberation Day March was important because it showed the public that LGBTQ people existed. Pride now is a weekend-long event in many cities, featuring parades, booths, and activist grassroots organizations.

PRIDE THROUGHOUT HISTORY

Throughout the 1970s and 1980s, Pride was meant to pressure government leaders for reform. Chants and political posters were common. In 1970, marchers shouted, "Say it clear, say it loud. Gay is good, gay is proud."[3] In the 1980s, as a crisis formed around the spread of human immunodeficiency virus (HIV) and acquired immunodeficiency syndrome (AIDS), marchers used signs to call on the government to help. One protester even taped his pill bottle to his overalls. Many people were afraid to talk about HIV and AIDS. The pill bottle demanded that people face the reality of the disease.

Throughout the 2000s, the focus of protests and Pride shifted to marriage equality. Chris Frederick, the managing director for NYC Pride, says that Pride events today are filled with families. He believes that Pride parades and marches reflect the social movements of the LGBTQ community at the time of the events. The Pride events of the 1970s focused on advancing employment equality. In the 1980s, the HIV/AIDS crisis became the focus. It wasn't until the 2000s that Pride became the celebration that we think of today.

DYKES ON BIKES AND THE RECLAMATION OF SLURS

Words such as *dyke* and *queer* can be seen as derogatory. These words have been used by non-LGBTQ people throughout history to bully and harass LGBTQ people. Over time, though, some people in the LGBTQ community have started to reclaim these words.

Dyke is often used as a slur toward lesbian and bisexual women. The group Dykes on Bikes started in 1976 in San Francisco. Approximately 25 women rode their motorcycles in the San Francisco Pride Parade.[4] The group of women soon formed an organization that originally was known as the Women's Motorcycle Contingent (WMC). However, within the larger San Francisco and LGBTQ community, the WMC began to be known as Dykes on Bikes. In 2007, the group sought to trademark its logo. Initially the US Patent Office rejected its request. It said that the group's name was derogatory. However, because Dykes on Bikes is self-referential and not degrading to an outside group, the group was allowed to keep its name and trademark.

Other related events, such as the Dyke March and Trans Day of Action (TDOA), are celebrated separately. Both of these events are focused on the political action that large gatherings of LGBTQ people can accomplish. The Dyke March does not allow businesses to sponsor it, and it doesn't receive permission from city officials. Messages during the march are politically and socially informed. In 2018, many of the signs called on legislators to release the detained immigrant children being held near the border between the United States and Mexico.

TDOA, also called Trans Day of Visibility, is a politically charged gathering for trans, nonbinary, and gender-nonconforming (GNC) people. In New York, the gathering happens on Pier 45, which is across from the Stonewall Inn. It is organized by TransJustice and the Audre Lorde Project. Fatima Jamal, a former communications coordinator for the Audre Lorde Project, said in 2018 that there are still many things that need to change. "Transgender and gender non-conforming people are getting killed, and . . . committing suicide," Jamal explained.[5] Nico Fonseco, program director for TransJustice, echoed Jamal, saying, "With [President Donald Trump's] administration and a lot of political things leaning toward the right, it's important that TDOA remains the space that it's always been."[6] TDOA allows people to build community and seek action from legislators.

AUDRE LORDE

Audre Lorde described herself as a "black, lesbian, mother, warrior, poet."[7] She was a child of immigrant parents and lived in New York. Lorde wrote extensively about the intersections of race, gender, sexuality, and class. She received many honors, including being named Poet Laureate of New York. Several of her books were published after her death in 1992. One of these was a collection of nonfiction essays, *Sister Outsider: Essays and Speeches*. The text is regarded as an important work in black feminist literature.

The Audre Lorde Project was started in 1994. It was brought about by Advocates for Gay Men of Color. They recognized that there was a need to bring together a community of people who shared similar experiences of discrimination.

MARCH ON WASHINGTON

In 1978, San Francisco supervisor and gay activist Harvey Milk called on the LGBTQ community to gather for a national demonstration inspired by the black civil rights movement in the 1960s. Milk was assassinated before the project came to fruition, but two New York activists, Joyce Hunter and Steve Ault, went forward with organizing a march on Washington.

Before he was assassinated, Milk asked gay artist and drag queen Gilbert Baker to create a symbol of pride for the LGBTQ community. Baker decided on a rainbow flag. He said, "Our job

After Harvey Milk was assassinated, LGBTQ people in San Francisco rioted in the streets.

as gay people was to come out, to be visible, to live in the truth. . . . A flag really fit that mission, because that's a way of proclaiming your visibility."[8] The flag was first flown at San Francisco Pride, but it didn't become recognizable as an LGBTQ symbol until 1994.

By marching on Washington, activists hoped to spark change and liberation for LGBTQ people throughout the United States. They also wanted to build a national community of LGBTQ activists that stretched beyond their cities or states. In the decades before the internet, collaboration was just as necessary but far more difficult to produce.

Activists called the 1979 March on Washington a success. Estimates on the number of people in attendance range from 25,000 to more than 100,000.[9] The crowd filled Pennsylvania Avenue as marchers walked past the White House and stopped at the Washington Monument,

EXPANDING THE RAINBOW FLAG

In 2017, the Office of LGBT Affairs in Philadelphia, Pennsylvania, unveiled a new Pride flag at the start of the city's Pride celebration. The new flag, a part of the More Color, More Pride campaign, added black and brown stripes to the top of the flag. The stripes are meant to recognize discrimination and violence against POC in the LGBTQ community. Sometimes this violence is perpetrated by white LGBTQ people. By giving voice to the nonwhite LGBTQ community, advocates hope a larger conversation will begin.

where a rally was held. Subsequent marches were held in 1987, 1993, 2000, 2009, and 2017. Each protest had a different focus, and each grew in size.

The 1987 march focused on the federal government's inaction in response to the AIDS epidemic. In 1993, the focus turned to presidential candidate Bill Clinton and activists' hope for what reforms he might bring for the LGBTQ community. Marchers wanted to change the restrictions on gay and lesbian people serving openly in the military. At the time, it was illegal for gay and lesbian servicepeople to be out while in the military.

One recent march occurred in 2017 after the inauguration of President Trump. In response to the Trump administration's

POLICE PRESENCE AT PRIDE

Throughout the 1980s and 1990s, gay New York police officers needed to fight their own department to be allowed to walk in the New York Pride March. They did not want to be fired. At that time, seeing police officers offered people a sense of hope and community. However, in the 2010s, police presence at Pride marches and parades has become a source of tension for Pride organizers and social justice groups. With the large number of POC killed every year by police, many participants in Pride don't see a police presence as a positive thing. Groups such as No Justice No Pride tried to block the police presence at New York Pride in 2017.

Some people believe that Pride should focus only on LGBTQ issues. LGBTQ officers often are excluded from their own community. Advocates for allowing police to march in the parades say that police at Pride are an important step toward building trust in the community.

The 1993 March on Washington ended at the National Mall.

decisions regarding immigration, trans rights, and disability rights, organizers of the march focused their attention on the marginalized voices of the LGBTQ community. This included POC. One of the attendees, Raffi Freedman-Gurspan, the director of external relations at the National Center for Transgender Equality, stated that she was "pleased to see that this march is focusing on marginalization."[10] The LGBTQ community started to look at whose voices were being heard. Many people recognized that LGBTQ people were also POC or came from different economic classes. These aspects, and others, form intersectional identities. Community members with these identities face different hardships than white, cis, gay men. It is important to consider the needs of everyone in the community.

DISCUSSION STARTERS

- Have you ever been to a Pride festival or seen news coverage or video from one? What was that experience like?

- Do you think Pride festivals are still a revolutionary act? Why or why not?

- Do events such as TDOA and the Dyke March help or hinder the goals of Pride?

4

FAMILY AND
COMMUNITY
ACCEPTANCE

As LGBTQ people choose to come out, or make their identity public, they can face a lot of stigma. The reactions from friends and families can be hurtful. Community views of LGBTQ issues directly influence LGBTQ people. LGBTQ support groups and organizations provide necessary resources for LGBTQ people and their loved ones.

PFLAG

In 1972, Jeanne Manford marched down the street with her gay son, Morty, in the Christopher Street Liberation Day March. Only a few months before, Jeanne and her husband found out their son was beaten up at a protest rally while police officers stood by and watched. Jeanne knew something had to be done. At the Christopher Street march, she held a sign up that read, "Parents of Gays: Unite in Support for Our Children."[1]

WE ARE

PFLAG
FAMILY!

I ♥ MY
DAUGHTER
& HER WIFE!
* MARRIED MARCH 15, 2013 * SEATTLE, WA *

PFLAG
TWIN CITIES

Eric Marcus, an author who writes about LGBTQ history, says there wasn't a precedent for this type of action. According to Marcus, "It's a little hard to imagine now what that period was like, how revolutionary it was for a parent to walk in the gay pride march in New York City."[2] Marchers and spectators alike also recognized the importance of this gesture. Gay men and lesbians approached Manford again and again. They asked her to please speak with their own parents.

Based on the overwhelming response to her presence, Manford decided to create a support group for parents of gay and lesbian children. On March 11, 1973, Jeanne and a group of 20 participants gathered in the basement of a Methodist church in Greenwich Village to form Parents, Families,

HOW ARE COMMUNITY ATTITUDES CHANGING?

Attitudes surrounding LGBTQ rights are shifting. But they aren't always shifting toward more acceptance. In 2017, a Harris Poll found that more people in the United States were uncomfortable around LGBTQ people than in 2016. The study found that 30 percent of respondents were uncomfortable to learn a relative was LGBTQ, up from 27 percent in 2016. An even larger percentage was uncomfortable knowing that their child had a lesson in LGBTQ history in school. Despite this, 79 percent of Americans believe LGBTQ people deserve to be treated equally. GLAAD president Sarah Kate Ellis says this increase could be due to a number of factors. She says there is a "misconception" that people in the LGBTQ community already have equal rights in the United States.[3]

and Friends of Lesbians and Gays (PFLAG).[4] For the next few years, other chapters of PFLAG formed in communities around the United States. After the 1979 March on Washington, leaders from PFLAG chapters met in Washington, DC, to discuss their goals. In 1982, chapter leaders created a national organization, the nonprofit Federation of Parents, Families, and Friends of Lesbians and Gays. PFLAG began distributing pamphlets and information to universities and faith communities, offering support and education for LGBTQ people and allies. PFLAG also created groups in rural areas where community acceptance of LGBTQ people tends to be lower. As of 2018, more than 400 PFLAG chapters existed around the United States. The organization has more than 200,000 members.[5] PFLAG provides a space for allies of LGBTQ children to share their experiences openly and find methods of support. Groups offer in-person meetings, online forums, and telephone hotlines.

THE TREVOR PROJECT

The Trevor Project started as a short film following a gay youth named Trevor who attempts suicide. The film, *Trevor*, was adapted from a stage production called *Word of Mouth*. It won an Academy Award. But as the film was receiving national attention, the director, Peggy Rajski, realized that a resource didn't exist for struggling LGBTQ youth. The Trevor Lifeline launched in 1998. It was a suicide hotline for youth in crisis.

Peggy Rajski started the Trevor Project to help LGBTQ youth struggling with thoughts of suicide.

Since then, the program has grown into the Trevor Project. It provides crisis counseling, research, training, and resources to help LGBTQ youth.

Suicide attempts among nonheterosexual youth are as much as five times more common than among heterosexual youth.[6] For trans youth, that rate is closer to ten times higher.[7] Several factors, such as family acceptance, peer support, and community support, influence suicide rates. LGBTQ youth face a higher risk for mental illness and suicide when support networks are hard to find. The Trevor Project is the leading LGBTQ youth suicide prevention organization in the United States.

PARENTAL SUPPORT

The amount of support that LGBTQ youth receive from their families directly influences their emotional well-being and hope for the future. LGBTQ youth who face a high level of rejection from family and caregivers are more than eight times as likely to attempt suicide. They have higher rates of depression and drug abuse. This can lead to other risky behaviors, such as unprotected sex. LGBTQ youth who are rejected by their parents are more than three times as likely to be at high risk for contracting a sexually transmitted infection (STI) and HIV. In addition, rejection or a lack of family support directly affects a youth's hope for the future. Ninety-two percent of youth with accepting families believe they can be happy as adults. However, only 35 percent of youth believe they can be happy if they came from families who did not accept their identities.[8]

MEDIA REPRESENTATION

LGBTQ youth look to TV and film to find representation. But sometimes the representation is negative or nonexistent.

Founded in 1985, GLAAD led the way for news media outlets to change the way they talked about LGBTQ issues. At the beginning of the AIDS crisis, news sources often cited the disease as a gay disease. The implication was that non-LGBTQ people couldn't contract HIV or AIDS. But that wasn't true, and the generalization caused panic to spread through cities.

In 1987, GLAAD worked with the *New York Times*. It convinced the *Times* to use the word *gay* instead of *homosexual* in news stories. Today, the GLAAD Media Reference Guide educates people on proper terminology to use when writing or reporting on LGBTQ issues.

GLAAD also advocates for diversity in television programming. It publishes two yearly reports. The first, "Where We Are On TV," monitors how many LGBTQ characters appear on scripted shows. The other, "Studio Responsibility Index,"

A BROADER SCOPE

GLAAD and PFLAG are two organizations that have chosen to keep their acronyms but not their names. PFLAG was originally named Parents, Family, and Friends of Lesbians and Gays. GLAAD used to stand for Gay and Lesbian Alliance Against Defamation. Over time, it became clear that these names could feel exclusionary to people in the LGBTQ community, even though the organizations were not. To be more inclusive and to broaden the outreach of the organization, PFLAG changed its name officially to just PFLAG. Similarly, GLAAD changed its name. People already recognized PFLAG and GLAAD as LGBTQ-affirming organizations. That is why they chose to get rid of the old names.

Stephanie Beatriz, *center*, plays the bisexual Latina character Rosa Diaz on *Brooklyn 99*. Beatriz, who is also bisexual, advocated for her character's sexuality to appear on the show.

ranks Hollywood studios based on several factors. It's not only about the sheer number of LGBTQ characters. The index also takes into account how those characters are treated and what types of films LGBTQ characters are found in. These reports allow GLAAD advocates to work with networks to create more inclusive and respectful depictions of LGBTQ characters. Better representation directly influences society's views of LGBTQ issues. "When people are able to see something represented, they are better able to understand and grasp who those

LGBTQ characters on television shows such as *Steven Universe* can inspire fans to cosplay, or dress up, as the characters at conventions.

people are," says Dr. Jennifer O'Brien, a clinical psychologist at the Massachusetts Institute of Technology.[9]

SAFE SCHOOLS

The Gay, Lesbian, and Straight Education Network (GLSEN) works toward creating safe schools for LGBTQ youth. It conducts a national school climate survey every two years. GLSEN also provides kits for teachers to create safe classrooms for LGBTQ students. The group compiles tips for students to start their own gay-straight alliances or gender-sexuality alliances (GSAs). GSAs are their own social movement. They rely on students to take control of the climate in their schools. GSAs believe in the power that youth have to create change.

GSAs may participate in several national events

GLSEN'S NATIONAL STUDENT COUNCIL

LGBTQ youth leaders from across the country are selected from a pool of applicants to serve on the National Student Council (NSC), sponsored by GLSEN. NSC members brainstorm outreach programs and interventions for the upcoming year at their schools. Charlie Peña and Katie Regittko, NSC members during the 2016–2017 year, became friends and supports for each other during their week as roommates as well as throughout the rest of the year. Peña and Regittko created the #ILoveBiself campaign for Bisexual Awareness Week. They also wrote an essay for *Teen Vogue*, and the #ILoveBiself hashtag was used hundreds of times on Twitter. Messages of support and self-love streamed in. One Twitter user wrote, "When I was 14 and came out as bisexual I would have loved to see a Twitter chat like #ILoveBiself."[10]

Some people wear signs or cover their mouths during the Day of Silence. Others may hold their hands in a shh gesture when asked to speak.

during the school year. One week in October is Ally Week. Ally Week is about education. GSAs want more people to identify as allies—as people who support their LGBTQ peers and friends. Groups may create an Ally Pledge.

The Day of Silence happens in April. It is a day when LGBTQ students and their allies don't speak. The silence of these students represents the ways in which homophobia and transphobia silence voices unknowingly. It also serves to illustrate the high rate of suicide that exists in the LGBTQ community.

GSAs are an important part of the larger LGBTQ social movement. Schools that are more accepting of LGBTQ students have lower rates of harassment. This, combined with visibility, has a similar effect to that of representation on television: a more accepting, understanding community.

DISCUSSION STARTERS

- Does your town have a PFLAG chapter? If it does, how do you think it affects your community? If it doesn't, how do you think your community would change if it had a chapter?

- How do you use social media to stay connected to your community? What are the pros and cons of social media?

- Does your school have a GSA? If it does, what are some ways the GSA supports LGBTQ youth? If it doesn't, how might your school change if it had a GSA?

SPOTLIGHT ON US OLYMPIAN ADAM RIPPON

Figure skater Adam Rippon rose to fame even before he won an Olympic medal at the 2018 Winter Games. Rippon was the first openly gay athlete on Team USA to win a medal at the Winter Olympics. As news of his identity spread, many headlines about Rippon referred to him as the "Gay Olympian." This created a level of visibility that hadn't been seen before in Olympics coverage. Rippon wanted to use that visibility to create change. Rippon hoped the attention would allow him to be an advocate and role model for LGBTQ youth. In an interview with GQ, Rippon said, "I know what it's like to be young and to feel like you don't belong. I always said that if I had the platform and the opportunity to share my story and make it easier for others, I would—so that, in a way, I can be the role model that I was looking for as a kid."[11]

Since the Olympics, Rippon has chosen to become more involved in helping LGBTQ youth. He started working with GLAAD's Youth Engagement Program. The program works with LGBTQ young people and their allies to create more accepting communities. While talking about working with youth, he said, "When I was young, to have had somebody out there to look up to . . . it would have made a world of difference, it would have changed my life."[12] Adam Rippon is helping to empower young people to create their own changes within their communities. The hope is that these changes will ripple into larger, nationwide policies.

Adam Rippon won a bronze medal at the 2018 Winter Games in Pyeongchang, South Korea.

5

ACT UP AND
THE AIDS CRISIS

HIV and AIDS attack the immune system in the body. Many people do not show signs of infection. After the initial flu-like symptoms go away, there is no definitive way to tell whether someone has HIV without a medical test. The virus multiplies while killing immune cells and lymph nodes that fight off foreign bodies. This compromises the immune system. It is easy for people with HIV or AIDS to become ill. The body has no way to protect itself. Ninety-eight percent of people with untreated HIV die of complications related to the virus.[1]

AIDS first came to the public's attention in the United States in 1981. At that time five gay men contracted a strain of pneumonia.[2] This particular strain of pneumonia almost never attacked healthy immune systems. In the following year, the *New York Times* published an article about a new immune system disorder. By that time, more than 330 cases had been diagnosed, and 136 of those people had died.[3] Doctors had

known for some time that HIV, the virus that causes AIDS, could infect any person regardless of sexual orientation. However, because of the disproportionate number of gay men affected, the condition became known as gay-related immune deficiency, or GRID. Even after the name was changed to AIDS, the public continued to describe the disease as the "gay plague."

This period in the 1980s is often referred to as the AIDS crisis. Although doctors understood where HIV/AIDS came from and how it was spread, they were unsure how to treat someone who could not fight infections. In addition, the public had little information on how to prevent the spread of HIV. Rumors claimed that HIV could be spread through using the same public toilets as someone with HIV, drinking out of the same water fountain, and even breathing the same air.

AIDS AROUND THE WORLD

HIV/AIDS continues to be a global issue. The highest prevalence is in eastern and southern Africa, where as many as one in 25 people live with HIV.[4] Higher rates of infection occur in lower-income areas. But these areas are also the last places to receive testing and treatment. In 2017, approximately 1.8 million people were newly infected with HIV around the world. Many of these infections came from breastfeeding mothers who passed the virus to their infants. Global health organizations work hard to get medication to these populations. In 2017, 80 percent of pregnant mothers with HIV were on these medications. Since the epidemic began, 35 million people globally have died from AIDS-related complications.[5]

US president Ronald Reagan was in office from 1981 to 1989, when the AIDS crisis was gaining momentum in the United States. HIV caused a lot of fear, and this fear promoted homophobia in the general public. By 1984, 4,200 people had died from AIDS-related complications.[6] However, journalists and doctors concerned with the epidemic were met with ridicule by the press secretary and the president's representatives. President Reagan did not say the word *AIDS* until 1985. The members of the LGBTQ community who lived through the AIDS crisis blame the Reagan administration for the deaths of thousands of people. Tom Ammiano, a school teacher and San Francisco school board member, went to more than 100 funerals in the first ten years of the epidemic. Remembering the

HIV cells attach to healthy cells in the body using glycoproteins. The virus then spreads from cell to cell.

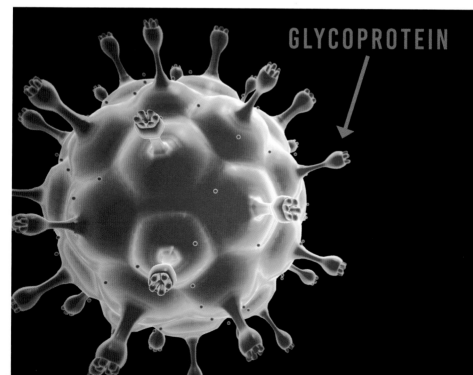

GLYCOPROTEIN

THE AIDS QUILT

In 1985, Cleve Jones, an activist in San Francisco, was at a candlelight march to honor the life of Harvey Milk. While Jones was there, he learned that more than 1,000 San Franciscans had died from AIDS-related complications. He knew then that something had to be done to remember these people. He handed out note cards and asked people to write the name of someone who had died. After he collected the cards, he taped them to the side of the San Francisco Federal Building. That image gave Jones an idea. Two years later, a small group of volunteers gathered in a storefront to begin a memorial to the people who had died. What grew out of this gesture is the AIDS memorial quilt. The quilt was first unveiled in Washington, DC, on October 11, 1987, and there were 1,920 panels. More than 500,000 people visited the National Mall to see the memorial. Every year the quilt grows. In 2018 there were more than 48,000 three-foot-by-six-foot panels, each dedicated to someone who was lost to AIDS-related illnesses. It has panels from every state and more than 28 countries. The quilt is rarely displayed all at once. Panels that are not on display around the country are archived in Atlanta, Georgia.[9]

Reagan presidency leaves "a very bitter taste that won't be forgotten," he says.[7]

By 1987, 10,000 New Yorkers had been infected with HIV, and approximately one-half of them had died.[8] People began holding meetings about what could be done about the crisis. Larry Kramer spoke at an event for a community lecture series. A week later, he spoke at another meeting in the same location. Three hundred people attended. Kramer helped create the AIDS Coalition to Unleash Power (ACT UP). This organization pressured the US government into action regarding the AIDS crisis. Word spread, and other chapters formed in large cities across the country. The group staged nonviolent, direct action protests to draw a lot of media attention. There were sit-ins

Larry Kramer helped create ACT UP. The organization uses the slogan "silence=death" to spread awareness of HIV/AIDS.

Any person, regardless of gender identity and sexuality, can contract HIV. Regular screenings for sexually transmitted infections (STIs) can help prevent the spread of HIV.

and marches. The protesters surrounded political buildings and the personal homes of homophobic politicians. The media attention that ACT UP received helped push change forward.

TREATMENT

Activists in the 1980s told the US Food and Drug Administration (FDA) that if there were a drug available to help treat HIV, it would be unethical not to release it to the public. HIV is a retrovirus. Drugs designed to work against this type of virus are known as antiretrovirals. An antiretroviral called AZT was approved for use in 1987 after a short study. There were many issues with AZT. The drug had dangerous side effects, and it was expensive. Patients paid approximately $8,000 per year.

Today, that would be equivalent to approximately $17,800 per year.[10] Critics claimed the pharmaceutical company prioritized profits over people's lives. The vast majority of people living with HIV were also living in poverty. However, from 1987 until the 1990s, AZT was the only antiretroviral option for people with HIV.

ACT UP was frustrated with the lack of research into treating HIV. The FDA took a long time to approve new HIV medications and often wouldn't allow people living with AIDS to participate in the drug trials. ACT UP worked to change that and fought

THE LOST GENERATION

Between 1988 and 1995, it is estimated that 78 percent of all deaths in people living with HIV were from AIDS-related complications. Many of these people were gay men between the ages of 25 and 50 years.[11] This demographic became known as the lost generation. The deaths had significant influences in the art, theater, and music industries, where many young gay men held careers. The LGBTQ community lost mentors and teachers. Howard Ashman, a songwriter on Disney musicals, died from AIDS-related complications. His collaborator Alan Menken said, "A certain world has been shattered. Especially in the gay community, people have been left with such a crater around them. . . . There went someone who could have been a director, a producer, who would have been a teacher to thousands of people."[12]

The generation of survivors today struggles to tell its stories, due in part to the stigma associated with the disease during the epidemic. Little research has been done to investigate the effects that so much loss might have on a person. Within the LGBTQ community, elders fear a loss of oral histories as youth try to navigate their way through a changing world. In addition, because of the lack of government involvement, a gap exists in the information that is available. A lot of information is missing from the history of HIV/AIDS in the LGBTQ community of the United States.

pharmaceutical companies to lower the price of AZT. The group gathered around the Department of Health and Human Services building. Eventually, the ACT UP New York Treatment & Data Committee created its own treatment agenda. If the government wouldn't do anything, then ACT UP decided to conduct its own research into HIV/AIDS. The Treatment & Data Committee presented its findings at the Fifth International AIDS Conference. Its research revolutionized the treatment of AIDS.

Between 1981 and 1987, the death rate for people with HIV was 95.5 percent.[13] By 2015, that rate had dropped significantly. In 2015, there were approximately 1.1 million people living with HIV. That year, approximately 6,500 people died from HIV-related causes, according to the CDC. That means the death rate in 2015 was approximately 0.5 percent.[14]

PREVENTING HIV

The AIDS Action Committee created the "Do It Daily" campaign for PrEP. PrEP is an effective preventative medication against contracting HIV. Campaigns are used to create a conversation surrounding an issue. Many people do not know about PrEP. HIV continues to be highly stigmatized in society. But this creates a culture of silence. Worse, it can promote the spread of misinformation. The "Do It Daily" campaign utilizes limited text and clear images of a pill bottle. The images show the bottle on a kitchen table with breakfast or in a bathroom next to a toothbrush. These images are used on purpose. There is nothing shameful about taking care of one's health. Just like a daily vitamin, PrEP should be taken every day.

Medication for HIV is much different as of 2018 than it was in 1987. Options available for people living with HIV are much more extensive. People who test positive for HIV are usually put on antiretroviral therapy (ART) to slow the progression of the infection. Sometimes, virus levels can become so low they are undetectable. Studies show that if a virus is undetectable, it is not transmittable.

Pre-exposure prophylaxis (PrEP) was approved by the FDA in 2012. PrEP is a daily medication. It lowers the risk of a person contracting HIV when taken consistently. In 2018, the FDA approved the medication for people between the ages of 15 and 17. PrEP and ART help people reduce the spread of HIV and live longer and healthier lives. Because of advances in medication, people with HIV in the United States rarely develop AIDS if they remain consistent with treatment. Advances in HIV/AIDS research and treatment would not be possible without social movements taking a stand against the government.

DISCUSSION STARTERS

- What did you know about HIV/AIDS before reading this chapter? Was there anything that you read that was surprising?

- Consider ACT UP's slogan, "silence=death." What do you think that means? What issues do people remain quiet about today? How could this silence be interpreted as violence?

6

MAKING A
FAMILY

I n 2000, the Human Rights Campaign (HRC) helped organize the Millennium March on Washington. This was the fourth major LGBTQ rights march since the first one in 1979. One of the poster campaigns for the march stated, "Protect Our Families." Organizers of the event wanted this march to be different. Instead of focusing on AIDS research or violence, organizers wanted this march to be a family event. Gay and lesbian couples marched together with the other protesters. They pushed their children in strollers. Couples carried their kids on their backs. One gay couple held a sign that said, "Keep Gay Adoption Legal." Elizabeth Birch was the executive director of the HRC at the time. She spoke with the crowd about her and her partner's adoption of twins. She said, "Don't let anybody tell you that you're not worthy of parenthood."[1]

In 2000, when the Millennium March was held, marriage equality didn't exist. Massachusetts, the first state to legalize

same-sex marriage, didn't do so until 2003. It wasn't until 2015, with the landmark US Supreme Court case *Obergefell v. Hodges,* that marriage equality became the law of the land. Many LGBTQ advocates believed that after the Supreme Court decision, same-sex couples would be treated exactly the same as other couples. The thinking went that adoption, fostering, and other avenues for making families for LGBTQ people would be the same as for non-LGBTQ people. However, for lesbian and gay couples, as well as for single LGBTQ people, there are still hurdles in the way of creating a family that many non-LGBTQ people do not have to face.

SECOND-PARENT ADOPTION

When heterosexual couples adopt a child, both people are listed on the adoption certificate. Same-sex couples do not have that same privilege. Many couples have to go through what is called a second-parent adoption after the first adoption or birth has already happened. In adoption circumstances, one parent adopts as a single parent, even if the couple is married. Then, the second parent petitions to adopt the child. This way both parents can share in the responsibility of raising the child.

Same-sex couples who choose in vitro fertilization (IVF) may also have to go through second-parent adoption. The spouse who carries the child is listed as the parent on the

Identification such as a birth certificate may contain spaces for the child's "father" and "mother." This can present problems if a same-sex couple uses IVF to have a child.

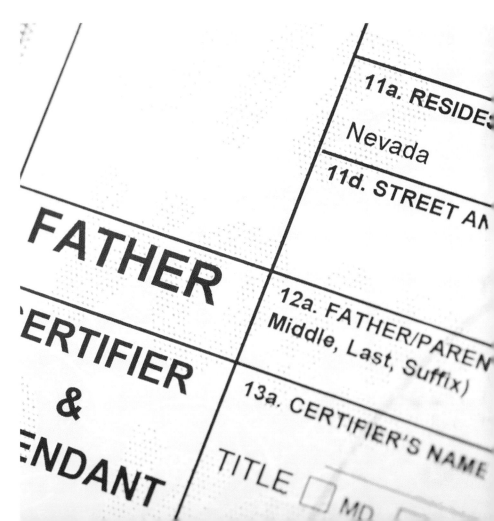

In 2010, Frank Martin Gill and his partner won a Florida court case that ended the state's ban on same-sex couples adopting children.

birth certificate. However, depending on the state, the second mother will need to formally adopt her child.

Joint adopting, where a couple adopts a child together, and second-parent adoption are important for the well-being of a child. If one of the spouses is not listed as a parent, that child could be forced to go into the foster system if something were to happen to the parent whose name is listed on the adoption or birth certificate.

ADOPTION AGENCIES

Kristy and Dana Dumont were married in 2011 and decided to start a family in 2016. They bought a house in Michigan with two spare bedrooms and a big backyard. They began looking at different adoption agencies in their county and contacted both Catholic Charities and Bethany Christian Services. They were excited to begin the process of expanding their family.

However, both organizations told them they didn't work with same-sex couples. The Dumonts were given a list of agencies that would work with them. However, all of the agencies were outside the county they lived in. They would have an hour-long drive each way to meet with social workers and attend classes. Neither thought that seemed right.

The couple contacted the American Civil Liberties Union (ACLU). Together with another lesbian couple, they sued the State of Michigan for discriminatory practices. In a statement, ACLU attorney Jay Kaplan said, "We are suing the state for

AMERICAN CIVIL LIBERTIES UNION

The ACLU was formed shortly after World War I. Since then, it has been an organization committed to defending individual freedoms of people in the United States. The ACLU has attorneys to represent clients in the courts. In recent history, more and more LGBTQ clients have turned to the ACLU for help.

The ACLU works to create social change through the court systems. Sometimes the most efficient way to change societal views is to change the law. Critics of the ACLU's methods claim that going through the court systems ignores the democratic process. They believe states should decide for themselves about laws pertaining to LGBTQ people.

allowing this practice. It does nothing for providing loving homes for children in need of them."[3]

Organizations such as the ACLU and the Family Equality Council are integral in creating change at the legislative level. But these organizations cannot make change without the families who are seeking equal treatment.

CARING PARENTS MAKE THE DIFFERENCE

A study from the Family Acceptance Project (FAP) found that family acceptance plays a larger role in LGBTQ-youth well-being than any other factor. Other factors are important to self-esteem and feelings of acceptance, researchers said, but no other factor better predicts youth resilience than acceptance from parents. Caitlyn Ryan, the director of FAP, explained that in the past the only resources for LGBTQ youth were peers and community members. "The impact of that perception," she says, "was several decades of not engaging families as a potential source of support for their LGBT children."[4] Family support helps build positive coping mechanisms and self-worth, key outcomes for a population that is at a much higher risk for suicide than their non-LGBTQ peers.

WHO IS HELPING THE KIDS?

LGBTQ youth are overrepresented in the foster system. Many LGBTQ-identified youth in the foster system are placed there because of family reactions to their sexualities or gender identities. Being placed in the foster care system is supposed to give these youth a sense of safety and security. But that doesn't always happen. They face challenges within the foster system that non-LGBTQ youth do not.

The Family Equality Council started the Every Child Deserves a Family (ECDF) Campaign in 2018. Ten states in the United States passed bills that allowed discrimination against LGBTQ people seeking to adopt or become foster parents. These bills didn't only discriminate against LGBTQ prospective parents. They also affected LGBTQ youth within the foster care system. The ECDF Campaign works to ensure that all children are placed in homes that provide care that is safe and understanding of the LGBTQ community.

John Paul Horn, who teaches child welfare policy in Boston, Massachusetts, grew up in the foster system. He described himself as "stereotypically" gay. In the foster system he faced harassment and bullying from his peers. His foster parents were not any better. They told him to keep his sexuality hidden. Of his foster mom, Horn remembered, "She was just like 'This is something that's not going to be acceptable here, and if this is who you are, then you just can't be here.'"[5]

Organizations such as the Family Equality Council and the ACLU help youth by connecting them with more families that are willing to adopt them. But what about those youth who never entered the foster system or ran away because conditions were so bad?

EFFECTIVE FAITH-BASED SHELTERS

The Covenant House is a collection of faith-based organizations. The organizations partner with the True Colors Fund, an LGBTQ advocacy group that works to end youth homelessness. Covenant House sites across the United States help organizations become more inclusive and welcoming to homeless youth from all backgrounds. Through multiple outreach programs, including a van program to deliver meals, crisis counseling, and ongoing care, youth who face homelessness are provided the support they need to build stability in their lives.

Although 40 percent of homeless youth identify as LGBTQ, organizations focused on helping youth have noted that access to safe shelter is limited.[6] Within the United States, most LGBTQ youth centers and homeless shelters are in large cities. But almost no resources exist for youth in rural areas and in the midwestern United States. Because of this, most homeless LGBTQ youth do not seek out assistance from LGBTQ-affiliated organizations. There simply are not enough organizations and shelters to accommodate the number of youth.

Some local groups have taken the issue of youth homelessness into their own hands. The Ali Forney Center in New York serves 1,400 LGBTQ youth through the drop-in center every year and serves 70,000 meals.[7] On a statewide scale, the Ali Forney Center advocates for the needs of homeless youth, including urging the governor to raise the age limit at which youth can no longer access emergency housing.

Running a program takes an incredible amount of time and money as well as dedicated personnel. The Zebra Coalition is located in Orlando, Florida. It reports that 18 percent of the US homeless youth population is located in Florida.[8] The coalition works with school administrators and students. It also provides shelter resources and a drop-in center. LGBTQ youth continue to face more homelessness than their non-LGBTQ peers. But with help from organizations such as the Ali Forney Center and the Zebra Coalition, many youth are able to gain stability in their communities.

DISCUSSION STARTERS

- Are you adopted, or do you know someone who is adopted? Have you or someone you know been in the foster care system? How do you think that experience has affected you or that person?

- How does your community view homelessness? What supports exist where you live, and what can be done to help people who are without homes?

- How do you think organizations such as the Ali Forney Center and the Zebra Coalition help with youth experiencing homelessness on a national scale, not just a local one?

The headquarters of the Human Rights Campaign is in Washington, DC.

HUMAN RIGHTS

Since the creation of the broader LGBTQ social movement, activists have referred to LGBTQ rights as human rights. The theme has been used by many social movements in the United States, including the African American civil rights movement in the 1960s. It has been a guide for many different organizations.

HUMAN RIGHTS CAMPAIGN

The Human Rights Campaign Fund (HRCF) was founded in 1980. Originally, it was a political action committee (PAC). The purpose of the PAC was to talk with candidates and endorse candidates who supported LGBTQ rights. The HRCF helped put LGBTQ issues in politicians' minds. An endorsement meant that many more LGBTQ people from the area would be likely to vote for that candidate.

In the HRCF's first election cycle in 1980, HRCF-endorsed candidate Jim Weaver, a Democrat from Oregon, won a seat in the House of Representatives. The HRCF soon set up offices

A CONTROVERSIAL ENDORSEMENT

In 2016, the HRC was criticized for endorsing a Republican nominee. Senator Mark Kirk of Illinois had a fairly good record for voting for pro-LGBTQ legislation, scoring a 78 on the HRC's Congressional Scorecard. The HRC defended its endorsement, saying, "The truth is we need more cross-party cooperation on issues of equality, not less. So when members of Congress vote the right way and stand up for equality . . . we must stand with them."[2] The organization believed it was important to recognize a Republican candidate who was fighting for LGBTQ rights. However, critics of the decision said that if Kirk was good, Kirk's Democratic opponent, Tammy Duckworth, was better. With a score of 100 on HRC's Congressional Scorecard, Duckworth was an LGBTQ advocate in addition to being a woman of color with a disability and a veteran of the Iraq War (2003–2011). Duckworth won the election.

in Washington, DC. By 1982, it was registered as a nonprofit political fund. The HRCF's funds allowed it to campaign for or against political candidates. During the 1982 election cycle, more than 80 percent of HRCF-endorsed candidates won their races. The HRCF was proven to be a political force. By 2005, that success rate grew to 90 percent.[1]

In 1995, a new executive director helped put the HRCF on a different path. Elizabeth Birch created a revised mission and vision for the HRCF. Part of that vision included officially dropping "Fund" from the title and calling itself the HRC. The expanded mission created an education and outreach branch. Such steps allowed the HRC to reach many more people than before.

ACCESS TO HEALTH CARE

For trans individuals in the United States, getting access
to health care is no easy task. The Affordable Care Act, a
health-care reform bill passed in 2010 under the Barack
Obama administration, included health-care protections for
transgender Americans. In 2017, the Trump administration
began challenging many of these protections. Several
organizations sued the Department of Health and Human
Services. They argued that treating trans patients violated their

After Trump's ban on transgender servicepeople went into
effect, people were unsure whether transitioning-related
health care would be covered for military dependents.

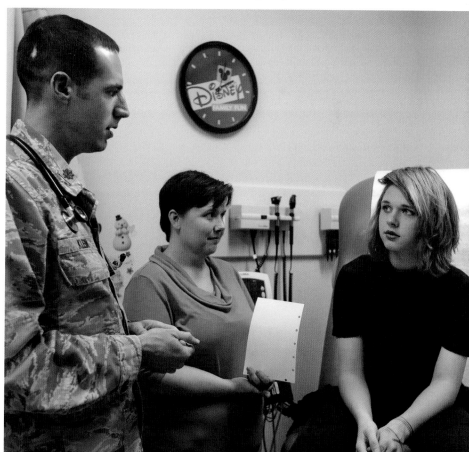

religious liberty. A Texas judge blocked the protections for trans people as the lawsuit moved forward. As a result, new guidelines for health organizations have been put into effect in several states. These guidelines allow practitioners and organizations to deny service and care to whole populations of people, including trans people.

Care doesn't necessarily include hormone replacement therapy or gender-affirming surgery, which many trans people

IS THE HRC DOING ENOUGH?

The HRC works hard to fight for equality for people in the LGBTQ community. Its website provides links and information to helpful resources across the United States. It is politically active and works to endorse candidates that will support LGBTQ-positive legislation. However, even organizations with the best intentions can miss the mark sometimes.

Many activists in the LGBTQ community believe that the HRC historically has ignored trans people in its lobbying for policy change. In 2007 the House of Representatives introduced the Employment Nondiscrimination Act (ENDA). Initially, the bill included gender identity as a protected class. However, concerns arose that the bill wouldn't pass with the inclusion of trans identities. A not-inclusive version was introduced in its place. The HRC was the only LGBTQ organization that continued to endorse the bill when gender identity was taken out of the proposed bill. Other LGBTQ organizations decided they would not support legislation that wasn't inclusive of trans and GNC identities. ENDA did not pass, and a national nondiscrimination policy has yet to be passed in Congress.

Today, the HRC continues to strive for diversity not only in Congress but also in its own organization. It has made progress in promoting trans people and POC to positions of authority. Even large, mainstream organizations can change with pressure from the community.

People in the LGBTQ community may avoid seeking health care because of previous negative experiences.

consider to be necessary aspects of their health care. Basic needs such as primary care and mental health care are denied to LGBTQ people. The Center for American Progress reported that 6 percent of nonheterosexual people were denied health care because of their sexual orientation in the previous year. Twenty-nine percent of transgender people were denied care by a doctor or nurse.[3] Studies show that LGBTQ people are less likely to seek out care when they fear discrimination. When LGBTQ people are denied care or given poor care, there can be serious repercussions for their health. For example, a doctor denied a patient his HIV medication when the patient disclosed that he had sex with other men. Another doctor turned away

THE NCLR'S SHANNON MINTER

Shannon Minter is a trans man. He was hired as the legal director for the National Center for Lesbian Rights. When the NCLR hired him, he had not yet transitioned. He transitioned later in life, when he was 35 years old. Minter is an active member of the LGBTQ rights community. He has worked on several important court cases, including a lawsuit against California's Proposition 8, which defined marriage as a union between one man and one woman. In 2015, President Barack Obama appointed Minter to the Commission on White House Fellowships. Minter interviewed and recommended fellows—yearlong paid assistants to senior White House staff—to President Obama. In a statement about the appointment, Minter said, "As a transgender man, I am especially grateful to President Obama for his commitment to building a government that reflects the full diversity of our country and for supporting equal opportunity for all people."[5]

an infant patient because her parents were lesbians.

CONVERSION THERAPY

The National Center for Lesbian Rights (NCLR) is a large organization in the United States dedicated to advancing LGBTQ rights though legal action. The NCLR was started in 1977 by Donna Hitchens. She was a lesbian just out of law school. Hitchens didn't want anyone else to feel afraid for their safety or freedom. The NCLR celebrated 40 years of service in 2017. Hitchens reflected on the years leading up to her starting the NCLR. She wrote, "It was decades before the Supreme Court marriage equality ruling. The Stonewall Riots had occurred only eight years earlier, and our identities were still seen by many as an illness or a crime."[4]

Today, the NCLR represents many court cases each year. These cases affect the legal landscape of LGBTQ civil rights and can cover topics such as reproduction, sports, youth and elder law, and transgender protections. One of NCLR's ongoing projects is working to end the practice of conversion, also known as ex-gay, therapy for LGBTQ people of all ages, but particularly youth.

Several major medical organizations, including the World Health Organization, the American Psychiatric Association, and the American Academy of Pediatrics, agree that not only is conversion therapy ineffective but it is harmful to recipients. Studies have shown that people who have undergone conversion

PROTESTS IN DETROIT

The Metro City Church outside Detroit, Michigan, faced backlash in February 2018. Activists protested outside the church after a program titled "Identity Workshop" was advertised on Facebook. The workshop was aimed at assigned-female-at-birth individuals who were "struggling with the thoughts that they are Trans – Bi – Gay – or other."[6] Pastor Jeremy Schossau asserted that this was not conversion therapy but did say Metro City was a "sexually traditionally-minded" church.[7]

Members of the LGBTQ community in Michigan held a protest outside of the church. Activists held posters with resources and encouraging messages for youth who were going to the meetings. This wasn't the first time Metro City Church was criticized for trying to convert an LGBTQ individual. A trans man said that in 2013, Schossau tried to exorcise him so that he wouldn't be trans anymore. Schossau denied the event ever took place.

The 2018 film *Boy Erased* follows Jared Eamons, *right*, as he attends conversion therapy in Arkansas.

therapy have an increased risk of depression, anxiety, and suicidality.

Because of the risk that conversion therapy poses to LGBTQ youth, NCLR is working closely with state organizations and lawmakers to create legislation to protect minors from the practice. In 2014, NCLR created the Born Perfect campaign. This campaign works with legislators to enact citywide or statewide bans on conversion therapy. As of January 2019, 15 states and Washington, DC, have banned the practice, and dozens more cities have created their own ordinances.[8] There is a long way to go before all LGBTQ youth are protected, but the Born Perfect campaign is a step in the right direction.

DISCUSSION STARTERS

- The HRC has a lot of political power. What areas of LGBTQ rights do you think it should focus on?

- Access to health care is important. What are some of the broader consequences for people who do not have reliable access to medical care?

- If it is clear that ex-gay therapy doesn't work, why do you think it still exists?

8

WHO GETS
TO BE LGBTQ?

Gatekeeping is a term used to describe the action of keeping a person or a group of people out of a location or group. Gatekeeping can be helpful or hurtful. Keeping a white student out of a group for African American students is a form of gatekeeping. This is done to give black students a voice. But within the LGBTQ community, gatekeeping is often used to exclude or discount the experiences of some LGBTQ people. These exclusionary acts can take many different forms. Some of them are as small as a word: a person who says only "real" women—meaning not trans—are allowed in a group. Or they might say that only people who are "actually" gay—meaning not bisexual—can join. Other exclusionary acts can evolve into physical altercations.

In the mid-1900s, groups such as the Mattachine Society and the Daughters of Bilitis were exclusive to create spaces for gay and lesbian people to feel safe. However, exclusion

was harmful to other people in the LGBTQ community. The Mattachine Society rarely allowed lesbians' input. Trans women were excluded from lesbian-only spaces such as the Daughters of Bilitis. Gatekeeping happens within the LGBTQ community both online and in person.

TRANS ERASURE

Trans Exclusionary Radical Feminists (TERFs) are people, mostly cisgender women, who exclude trans people from the fight for equality. People who are TERFs promote dangerous stereotypes about trans people. These include referring to trans women as men in dresses and referring to trans men as butch lesbians who suffer from internalized misogyny. Although TERFs are not an organization, they have created organizations such as Gender Identity Watch (GIW). GIW spreads misinformation about trans women.

WHY DOESN'T THE "A" STAND FOR ALLY?

There are several expanded acronyms for the LGBTQ community. One of those is the LGBTQIA—the lesbian, gay, bisexual, transgender, queer, intersex, and asexual—community. Sometimes, people say that the *A* stands for *ally*—someone who supports LGBTQ people. But this is a misinterpretation of the purpose of the acronym. The acronym serves to include people who have a different sexual or gender identity than the accepted norm. Thus, including the ally identity instead of asexuality isn't necessary.

Trans women have been at the forefront of many social movements within the LGBTQ community.

When organizations such as GIW become vocal, there can be repercussions for trans people.

In 2013, GIW partnered with the Pacific Justice Institute (PJI), an antigay religious freedom organization. Their actions prevented a trans student at a Colorado high school from accessing the girl's bathroom. The press release was titled, "Nightmare: Teen Boy Harasses Girls in Their Bathroom, Colo. School Tells Girls They Have No Rights."[1] This interpretation of events is inflammatory and degrading. Further, the actions of PJI and GIW led to an increase in bullying. The student was put

By listening to underrepresented voices in the LGBTQ community, others can help stop the erasure of certain groups.

on suicide watch in the weeks following the incident. Trans students already face higher rates of bullying and harassment in school. But research shows that inclusive school policies create a safer, healthier school environment. Trans students whose names and pronouns are respected tend to be less anxious and depressed.

Despite the crucial role that trans people, and more specifically trans women of color, have played in the LGBTQ rights movement, they are often ignored in discussions about equality. They face higher rates of violence from non-LGBTQ people. The 2015 US Transgender Survey found that 54 percent of respondents reported being victims of intimate partner violence.[2] The national average ranges from 25 percent to 33 percent.[3] Nearly one in ten trans respondents said that in the last year they had been physically assaulted, and almost half had been verbally assaulted.[4]

But even their own community has gone so far as to consider dropping the *T* from LGBTQ altogether. An article published in *Instinct* magazine asserted that issues for trans people were different from those for nontrans people. Therefore trans people shouldn't be included in the population of lesbian, gay, and bisexual people. The idea that the LGBTQ movement shouldn't include trans people is regarded by some as logical, whereas others say it's rooted in transphobia. Proponents of dropping the *T* say that it

MICHIGAN WOMYN'S MUSIC FESTIVAL

In 1976, a group of radical feminists founded the first annual Michigan Womyn's Music Festival, or MichFest. The weeklong celebration featured music and community building. However, the gathering came under scrutiny due to its "womyn-born-womyn" policy.[5] In 1991, a trans woman was thrown out of the festival after a group found out she was trans. By 2014, some artists decided to pull out of the festival because of the policy. In its fortieth year, MichFest announced that 2015 would be its last season. Some people celebrated the end of what they considered an exclusionary gathering, whereas others mourned the loss of what they saw as a rare opportunity to build community.

would get legislation through state and federal houses faster, allowing greater strides in the LGB movement.

However, opponents of the proposal say that while gender and sexual orientation are different, it is precisely because of this that the *T* should stay. Transgender people, especially trans women of color, face significantly higher rates of violence, homelessness, and poverty than their cisgender peers. Any not-inclusive legislation that passes would make it even harder in the future to pass transgender protections.

CONSEQUENCES OF ERASURE

Within the LGBTQ community, certain identities are deemed less important than other identities. Bisexual, asexual, and nonbinary people all face stigma within the LGBTQ community.

Bisexual people often say they have been told they're only half gay or are in denial about their actual sexual orientation. Further, people who perpetuate these ideas also spread the lie that bisexual people's orientation changes based on the gender of their current partner. According to this misconception, a bisexual man dating another man is gay until he starts dating a woman. Then he's straight. Such notions ignore the fluidity of identity and attraction and reinforce harmful stereotypes.

For many of the same reasons as bisexual people, asexual people face misunderstandings. Asexual, or ace, people have no sexual attraction to anyone, or may only have a limited sexual attraction to others. They are told their orientation isn't real—that everyone must have some sort of sexual attraction. These comments alienate asexual people who already feel stigmatized for their orientation. Asexual people are pathologized by the medical community. When they can't find support from either the medical community or their own LGBTQ community, many asexual people leave the movement altogether.

Asexual people aren't alone. Nonbinary people also often leave the mainstream LGBTQ movement to find support elsewhere. Nonbinary people have a gender identity that is sometimes both male and female, or neither male nor female. Cisgender people more easily accept or understand binary trans people. Trans women and trans men who are able to pass,

LOG CABIN REPUBLICANS

The Log Cabin Republicans (LCR) is the largest organization for conservative LGBTQ people. Founded in 1978, the LCR believes that the denial of LGBTQ rights isn't supported by the values of the Republican Party, also referred to as the Grand Old Party (GOP). When President Trump announced that transgender people were going to be excluded from the military, LCR condemned the policy. LCR President Gregory T. Angelo released a statement, saying, "Excommunicating transgender soldiers only weakens our readiness; it doesn't strengthen it."[6] It is the group's goal, working through grassroots chapters across the United States and in its national office in Washington, DC, to change the minds of GOP politicians. It believes "inclusion wins" and that a more inclusive GOP will also mean a stronger GOP.[7]

or be perceived as cisgender, are often hailed as the ideal for trans identities. But not all trans people can or want to pass in everyday society. Many LGBTQ people think it shouldn't matter—no one should have to prove their identity.

KEEPING PEOPLE IN

Blogs and online support forums provide resources for those who are looking. Gregory Ward runs the website Bisexual. He is also the founder of Fluid Arizona, which is a bisexual positivity group found on social media sites.

The Asexual Visibility and Education Network (AVEN) is an online support and education resource for asexual people and their allies. AVEN currently has more than 111,000 members.[8]

There are forums for people to engage in discussions as well as find an online community. These communities foster dialogue. They allow people to explore their sexual or asexual identities. These forums might include posts meant for older asexual people or for people who are looking to talk about the intersections of asexuality and gender.

People in the LGBTQ community recognize the importance of creating identity-specific spaces. They allow for community building and provide vital, affirming information for people. It is through this continued dialogue—often within and between online groups—that gatekeeping can become less ingrained in the LGBTQ community.

DISCUSSION STARTERS

- Where might you see gatekeeping in your everyday life? How does gatekeeping help or hurt people you know?

- What are some steps you can take to become a more understanding and welcoming person, even to those people you either don't understand or don't agree with?

- Think of a time in your life when you excluded someone from a group. What were your reasons for doing that? Reflecting now, would it have been helpful or hurtful to include them?

After the 2016 mass shooting at the Pulse nightclub in Orlando, Florida, Gays Against Guns organized die-ins to protest current gun control laws.

THE FUTURE OF
SOCIAL MOVEMENTS

n the past, social movements relied heavily on large cities, mailing lists, and word of mouth for events. But today, fewer and fewer people find out about events from fliers posted on bulletin boards. Word of mouth is replaced by the click of a button. Facebook invites, Instagram stories, and Twitter feeds give activists young and old the information they need. Social media also provides movements with nationwide reach, even to those people who don't live near metropolitan areas. LGBTQ advocates are able to reach thousands of people thanks to social media.

MEDIA REPRESENTATION AND ACTIVISM

Not all people call themselves, or want to be called, activists. There are many people for whom activism in the traditional sense—protesting outside of buildings or organizing marches

and people—is overwhelming or unsafe. But in an increasingly interconnected world, people are able to take some measure of ownership over social movements. Social media campaigns and online posting about topics people care about shape mainstream media and political ideologies.

The trope in television shows of killing off LGBTQ characters is known as "bury your gays."[1] Mental health professionals say that the practice of killing LGBTQ characters can affect youth far beyond a feeling of sadness. Research shows that "good representations are validating and normalizing for LGBTQ+ youth, and contribute to their identity development and overall well-being," says Lauren McInroy, a social work doctoral candidate at the University of Toronto.[2] Further, by

The cartoon *Steven Universe* features many LGBTQ characters.

actively showing the deaths of role models on television, the effects can be devastating, says Eve Ng, a professor at Ohio University. Ng states, "It reinforces this sense that LGBT people are second-rate."[3] Social movements work to create social equality for all people. When LGBTQ people feel they are less than non-LGBTQ people, communities should rally together to create change.

WHITEWASHING AND ERASURE IN MEDIA

Historically, Hollywood doesn't have an inclusive track record. Producers often cast white actors and put them in stereotypical makeup and costumes to portray POC. For much of the 1900s, these casting choices were common. In the 2000s, overt examples of racism have dwindled. However, discrimination continues to be an issue in mainstream media. Whitewashing—casting a white actor to play the role of a person of color—continues to be a common occurrence.

For movies depicting LGBTQ people and movements, this whitewashing and erasure denies the reality of history. Many LGBTQ social movements began because of the actions of trans women of color. To ignore that is to rewrite history.

As of the end of 2018, more than 200 lesbian and bisexual women characters have died on television shows.[4] After the death of the character Lexa on *The 100,* fans took to Twitter. They demanded better. In addition to creating a hashtag campaign, #LGBTfansdeservebetter, they also raised money for the Trevor Project. Jason Rothenberg, a producer of *The 100*, lost 10,000 Twitter followers in the week after Lexa's death.[5]

Some people fear that so much backlash could make white, straight, male writers and producers stop featuring LGBTQ characters. But activists say that there is a simple solution: hire diverse writers. People write characters that resemble themselves. Tumblr and other blog platforms have huge groups of writers reimagining the endings of shows. On these platforms, characters are reborn as LGBTQ, as people of different races or ability levels, and much more. The effect of more diverse television and film is that media reflects the actual diversity of the world.

INTERSECTIONALITY

Throughout the LGBTQ rights movement in the United States, the focus has been primarily on white, gay, cisgender men. Activists today are stressing the importance of shifting focus to other identities in the LGBTQ movement. For the vast majority of the LGBTQ community, sexual orientation is informed by other identities, including race, gender, disability, and economic status. Although white gay men celebrated after the Supreme Court decision legalizing same-sex marriage, other members of the community saw little change in how they interacted with societal pressures. A black trans woman still had to overcome transphobia, sexism, and racism.

The term *intersectionality* was first coined in 1989 by Kimberlé Crenshaw to refer to the experience of being both black and a woman.[6]

Since its creation, the definition of intersectionality has broadened. All identities and all sources of oppression are interconnected. That understanding must inform the LGBTQ movement to ensure that all LGBTQ people are being served in advocating for social and legal reform.

LGBTQ groups such as No Justice, No Pride (NJNP) have a history of blocking Pride parades as a form of protest. NJNP wants to disrupt the celebratory nature of Pride to remind people in the LGBTQ community about other injustices that people face. NJNP works out of Washington, DC. Its members are mostly POC and/or in the trans community. Groups such as NJNP take intersectionality seriously. The group recognizes that all voices are valuable in the discussion about

THE EVOLUTION OF INTERSECTIONALITY

When Kimberlé Crenshaw first used the term *intersectionality,* she was referring specifically to the experiences of working black women. For many years, the word lived almost exclusively in academic circles and retained its narrow definition. However, when intersectionality left academia, the word expanded and evolved to encompass a much broader experience. It has since been used in political circles and social justice groups. People discuss whether different pieces of media are intersectional. Writer Kristin Moe describes the shift in meaning this way: "The term has evolved from a way of describing the problem—the interactions between different forms of oppression—to a way of describing the solution."[7] Some people have claimed it's just a buzzword. But that buzzword has also created more inclusively minded organizations.

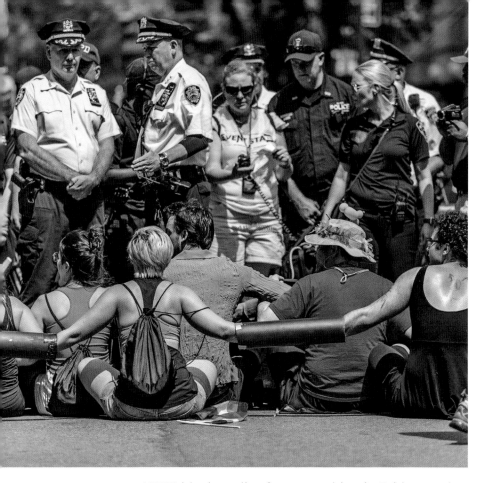

NJNP blocks police from marching in Pride parades.
Members link their arms together to stop people.

what equality looks like. No one voice or experience should be weighted more heavily than others.

NJNP is often met with criticism and sometimes even violence from the LGBTQ community. However, advocates for intersectionality say that this is not the time to be polite. Lourdes Hunter, executive director of the Trans Women of Color Collective, said, "When black trans women are murdered in the street, it doesn't happen in a polite manner. . . . When someone has their foot on your neck, you don't tap them and say, 'Excuse me.'"[8] Further, activists cite the history of using nonviolent, direct action protest strategies within the LGBTQ movement. Darnell Moore, a black gay man and an organizer for Black Lives Matter, noted that in the 1980s and 1990s, AIDS activists chained themselves to government buildings and performed die-ins in the streets. None of this was convenient, polite, or quiet.

HIGHLIGHTING TRANS VOICES

Between 2017 and 2019, the Trump administration enacted several directives that could harm trans people. From banning trans soldiers to redefining gender as unchangeable

CALLING FOR CHANGE AFTER TRAGEDY

On June 12, 2016, in the early hours of the morning, a gunman entered Pulse, an LGBTQ nightclub in Orlando, Florida. He opened fire on the people in the club. Forty-nine people died, and the shooting became one of the worst mass shootings in US history. In the aftermath of the shooting, many people donated blood. However, gay and bisexual men were turned away from blood banks.

The FDA placed bans on blood donations by gay and bisexual men in 1983 because of a fear of HIV. However, scientific evidence no longer supports a ban due to improvements in blood testing over time. LGBTQ activists and many legislators called on the FDA to lift the discriminatory ban entirely. "Gay Blood Drives" were created in protest. Gay and bisexual men brought straight friends who were willing to donate blood in their place. Protests happened on college campuses. One student at the University of Texas said, "After the shooting at the Pulse nightclub, a lot of queer men were like 'This is directly affecting my community, I want to help any way I can.'"[9] Despite protests, the FDA has not changed its policy as of January 2019.

ACCESSIBILITY IN THE LGBTQ COMMUNITY

In recent years, the LGBTQ movement has been criticized for using venues inaccessible to community members with disabilities. For LGBTQ people in wheelchairs, many venues don't have ramps. Other events may take place in bars or clubs. For people with autism, there could be too much stimulation. Deaf LGBTQ people rarely have interpreters or captions available to them. Some disabled LGBTQ people are saying that the exclusion is creating rifts within the movement. Umber Ghauri, a makeup artist based in London, United Kingdom, says that her experience coming out was one of isolation. Her further identities only made that isolation more extreme. In an article published in the *Independent*, Ghauri writes, "When you come out as LGBTQ+, you might experience isolation. . . . When you come out as disabled and LGBTQ+, the pool of people you share identities with becomes smaller."[11]

She goes on to write that accommodations for people with different ability levels are often an afterthought, if they are a thought at all. Issues like this drive disabled LGBTQ people away from the abled community. Ghauri urges LGBTQ people to consider the accessibility of every event.

from birth, the administration has sparked a rise in trans social movements. Across social media people rallied under hashtags such as #transbantweetup and #wewillnotbeerased. Actress and trans woman Laverne Cox stated, "Let's all come together and send the message to trans Americans that despite what this president and administration proclaims, that trans lives, safety, and service are valuable, that they matter."[10]

The narrative of the LGBTQ movement is one of diversity. LGBTQ people have varied experiences. They come from all racial, religious, and socioeconomic backgrounds. They are autistic, deaf, and paraplegic. They are military veterans and immigrants. Differences in sexual or gender identity do not mean there are no shared lived experiences. Highlighting difference is what makes the voices of the LGBTQ community so rich. But it is also the thing that needs to be fought most for.

Future LGBTQ social movements must not rely on the people who have the advantages. From Stonewall to the present day, social movements have always sprung out of a need for change and have been led by the people at the bottom. According to Sylvia Rivera, "I believe that's what brought [Stonewall] around. You get tired of being just pushed around. We are people. We are gay people."[12]

DISCUSSION STARTERS

- What can you do to start creating change in your community? Think about how these social movement groups began, and consider your own goals for equality.

- How can you work to lift up unheard voices in your school or town?

- How does disruption create change? What can you disrupt in your daily life?

ESSENTIAL FACTS

SIGNIFICANT EVENTS

- In 1969, LGBTQ people fought back against police during a raid of the Stonewall Inn. The weeklong uprising sparked the modern-day LGBTQ rights movement.

- Pride festivals happen throughout the United States and around the world. A Pride march or parade usually accompanies the festival.

- Between 1982 and the mid-1990s, thousands of LGBTQ people died during the AIDS crisis. The United States government was slow to act. A group of activists in New York and around the country formed ACT UP to protest.

KEY PLAYERS

- Sylvia Rivera and Marsha P. Johnson were revolutionary trans women during the surge of activism happening in New York after the Stonewall riots. Both were women of color and called for intersectionality from the beginning of the LGBTQ rights movement. Together, they founded STAR, an organization for homeless LGBTQ youth and sex workers.

- Shannon Minter is a trans man and legal director for the National Center for Lesbian Rights. He was then appointed to the Obama administration's fellowship recruiting program, becoming the first trans man to hold the position.

- Jeanne Manford founded PFLAG in 1973 and became a vocal advocate for LGBTQ people throughout the United States. PFLAG has more than 400 chapters and more than 200,000 members, providing support and resources for parents and LGBTQ individuals.

IMPACT ON SOCIETY

Social movements advocate for LGBTQ rights. Because of these movements, same-sex marriage is legal in all 50 states, treatments for HIV/AIDS are now widely available, and LGBTQ people can exist openly in government jobs. However, there is still a long way to go for LGBTQ rights. While nonheterosexual people can serve openly in the military, as of January 2019, trans people are banned from serving in the military. Only 15 states and Washington, DC, ban conversion therapy for minors. And by January 2019, several states had introduced bills that would allow discrimination against LGBTQ people.

QUOTE

"When people are able to see something represented, they are better able to understand and grasp who those people are."

—*Dr. Jennifer O'Brien, clinical psychologist at the Massachusetts Institute of Technology.*

GLOSSARY

ANTIRETROVIRAL
A medication used for people with HIV to slow the progression of the disease.

CISGENDER (CIS)
Having a gender identity that matches the sex they were assigned at birth.

DIRECT ACTION
A form of public protest that uses a person or group's power to achieve social change.

GENDER-AFFIRMING SURGERY
A type of surgery sometimes referred to as sex reassignment. This medical procedure is used by some trans people to feel more comfortable in their bodies by changing the appearance of physical sex characteristics. This term shifts frequently but is widely used as of 2019.

HOMOPHOBIC
Having a prejudice against someone who is lesbian, gay, or bisexual because of their sexual orientation.

HORMONE REPLACEMENT THERAPY
A drug regimen for some trans people that introduces estrogen or testosterone into the body to change its appearance.

INTERSECTIONALITY
Overlapping forms of oppression based on race, gender, class, sexuality, and other factors.

LYMPH NODE
A structure in the human body that filters harmful substances. When lymph nodes are attacked, their ability to filter out those substances is compromised.

NONBINARY
Having a gender identity that is neither male nor female, or sometimes both male and female.

PHARMACEUTICAL
Having to do with medications and their production and sale.

PRECEDENT
An earlier event or action that is regarded as an example to be considered in later similar circumstances.

PREVALENCE
How widely present something is.

PRIDE
An annual parade or protest for LGBTQ rights.

REFORM
A change.

TRANSGENDER (TRANS)
Having a gender identity that does not match the sex they were assigned at birth.

ADDITIONAL RESOURCES

SELECTED BIBLIOGRAPHY

Fitzsimons, Tim. "Police at Pride? Gay Cops, LGBTQ Activists Struggle to See Eye-to-Eye." *NBC News*, 23 June 2018. nbcnews.com. Accessed 10 Sept. 2018.

Lopez, German. "The Reagan Administration's Unbelievable Response to the HIV/AIDS Epidemic." *Vox*, 1 Dec. 2016. vox.com. Accessed 12 Sept. 2018.

Pasulka, Nicole. "Ladies in the Streets: Before Stonewall, Transgender Uprising Changed Lives." *NPR*. 5 May 2015. npr.org. Accessed 5 Sept. 2018.

FURTHER READINGS

Harris, Duchess, and Rebecca Rowell. *Growing Up LGBTQ*. Abdo, 2020.

Madrone, Kelly Huegel. *LGBTQ: The Survival Guide for Lesbian, Gay, Bisexual, Transgender, and Questioning Teens*. 3rd ed. revised. Free Spirit, 2018.

ONLINE RESOURCES

To learn more about LGBTQ social movements, please visit **abdobooklinks.com** or scan this QR code. These links are routinely monitored and updated to provide the most current information available.

MORE INFORMATION

For more information on this subject, contact or visit the following organizations:

AMERICAN CIVIL LIBERTIES UNION
125 Broad St., Eighteenth Floor
New York, NY 10004
aclu.org

The American Civil Liberties Union (ACLU) is a nonprofit organization that advocates for human rights through lobbying and court cases.

GLSEN
110 William St., Thirtieth Floor
New York, NY 10038
glsen.org

GLSEN is an advocate for LGBTQ students in the United States. It has resources for schools to be more welcoming and supportive of students.

STONEWALL NATIONAL MONUMENT
Intersection of Christopher, Grove, and Fourth Streets
New York, NY 10014
nps.gov/ston/index.htm

The Stonewall National Monument is the first national monument dedicated to LGBTQ people and the fight for civil rights.

SOURCE NOTES

CHAPTER 1. THE STONEWALL RIOTS

1. Lucian K. Truscott IV. "The Real Mob at Stonewall." *New York Times*, 25 June 2009, nytimes.com. Accessed 7 Jan. 2019.

2. Garance Franke-Ruta. "An Amazing 1969 Account of the Stonewall Uprising." *Atlantic*, 24 Jan. 2013, theatlantic.com. Accessed 7 Jan. 2019.

3. "Stonewall Riots." *History*, 31 May 2017, history.com. Accessed 7 Jan. 2019.

4. Truscott, "The Real Mob at Stonewall."

5. Nicole Pasulka. "Ladies in the Streets: Before Stonewall, Transgender Uprising Changed Lives." *NPR*, 5 May 2015, npr.org. Accessed 7 Jan. 2019.

6. Pasulka, "Ladies in the Streets."

7. Franke-Ruta, "An Amazing 1969 Account of the Stonewall Uprising."

8. Mey Valdivia Rude. "How Dare They Do This Again: Stonewall Veteran Miss Major on the 'Stonewall' Movie." *Autostraddle*, 10 Aug. 2015, autostraddle.com. Accessed 7 Jan. 2019.

9. Rude, "How Dare They Do This Again."

10. "Y'all Better Quiet Down." *Video Activism*, July 2012, videoactivism.net. Accessed 7 Jan. 2019.

11. Katia Hetter and Kevin Liptak. "Obama Names First National Monument to LGBT Rights." *CNN*, 24 June 2016, cnn.com. Accessed 7 Jan. 2019.

CHAPTER 2. BEFORE AND AFTER STONEWALL

1. "LGBT History on Governors Island." *National Park Service*, 26 Feb. 2015, nps.gov. Accessed 7 Jan. 2019.

2. Jeremy W. Peters. "The Decline and Fall of the 'H' Word." *New York Times*, 21 Mar. 2014, nytimes.com. Accessed 7 Jan. 2019.

3. Will Roscoe. "Mattachine: Radical Roots of the Gay Movement." *FoundSF*, n.d., foundsf.org. Accessed 7 Jan. 2019.

4. David G. Savage. "Supreme Court Faced Gay Rights Decision in 1958 over 'Obscene' Magazine." *Los Angeles Times*, 11 Jan. 2015, latimes.com. Accessed 7 Jan. 2019.

5. "Justia Opinion Summary and Annotations." *Justia*, n.d., supreme.justia.com. Accessed 7 Jan. 2019.

6. Savage, "Supreme Court Faced Gay Rights Decision in 1958 over 'Obscene' Magazine."

7. "Street Transvestite Action Revolutionaries Found STAR House." *NSWP*, n.d., nswp.org. Accessed 7 Jan. 2019.

CHAPTER 3. MARCHES AND PRIDE PARADES

1. Yohana Desta. "The Evolution of the Pride Parade, from Somber March to Celebration." *Mashable*, 19 June 2014, mashable.com. Accessed 7 Jan. 2019.

2. "Christopher Street Liberation Day 1970." *New York Public Library*, n.d., nypl.org. Accessed 7 Jan. 2019.

3. Desta, "The Evolution of the Pride Parade, from Somber March to Celebration."

4. "Our History." *Dykes on Bikes*, n.d., dykesonbikes.org. Accessed 7 Jan. 2019.

5. Eva Reign. "At Trans Day of Action, Attendees Came Together to Refocus Pride." *Them*, 24 June 2018, them.us. Accessed 7 Jan. 2019.

6. Reign, "At Trans Day of Action, Attendees Came Together to Refocus Pride."

7. "Audre Lorde." *Poetry Foundation*, n.d., poetryfoundation.org. Accessed 7 Jan. 2019.

8. Paola Antonelli. "MoMA Acquires the Rainbow Flag." *Inside/Out*, 17 June 2015, moma.org. Accessed 7 Jan. 2019.

9. Lou Chibbaro Jr. "Our History of Marching on Washington." *Washington Blade*, 11 June 2017, washingtonblade.com. Accessed 7 Jan. 2019.

10. Jenna Gray. "At Equality March, Thousands Rally for LGBTQ Rights." *PBS*, 11 June 2017, pbs.org. Accessed 7 Jan. 2019.

CHAPTER 4. FAMILY AND COMMUNITY ACCEPTANCE

1. Paula Sinclair. "Jeanne Manford: The Jewish Woman Who Advocated for Her Gay Son." *My Jewish Learning*, 8 June 2015, myjewishlearning.com. Accessed 7 Jan. 2019.

2. Lily Percy. "Jeanne Manford: A Mother First, Gay Rights Activist Second." *NPR*, 12 Jan. 2013, npr.org. Accessed 7 Jan. 2019.

3. Susan Miller. "Tolerance Takes a Hit: Americans Less Accepting of LGBT People in 2017, Survey Shows." *USA Today*, 25 Jan. 2018, usatoday.com. Accessed 7 Jan. 2019.

4. "Our Story." *PFLAG*, n.d., pflag.org. Accessed 7 Jan. 2019.

5. "Our Story."

6. "Facts about Suicide." *Trevor Project*, n.d., thetrevorproject.org. Accessed 7 Jan. 2019.

7. Laura Ungar. "Transgender People Face Alarmingly High Risk of Suicide." *USA Today*, 16 Aug. 2015, usatoday.com. Accessed 7 Jan. 2019.

8. Caitlyn Ryan. "Helping Families Support Their Lesbian, Gay, Bisexual, and Transgender (LGBT) Children." *National Center for Cultural Competence*, 2009, nccc.georgetown.edu. Accessed 7 Jan. 2019.

9. Jennifer O'Brien. "Why Visibility Matters." *Psychology Today*, 14 Nov. 2017, psychologytoday.com. Accessed 7 Jan. 2019.

10. "This LGBTQ Youth Leadership Program Changed Us and the World." *GLSEN*, n.d., glsen.org. Accessed 7 Jan. 2019.

11. @elielcruz. "When I was 14 and came out as bisexual I would have loved to see a twitter chat like #ILoveBISelf." *Twitter*, 23 Sept. 2016, 6:16 p.m. twitter.com. Accessed 7 Jan. 2019.

12. Jay Willis. "Olympian Adam Rippon Doesn't Care What Mike Pence (Or Anyone Else) Has to Say." *GQ*, 9 Feb. 2018, gq.com. Accessed 7 Jan. 2019.

13. Stephen Daw. "Adam Rippon Talks Being a Role Model for LGBTQ Youth & Crushing on Shawn Mendes on 'Ellen.'" *Billboard*, 1 Mar. 2018, billboard.com. Accessed 7 Jan. 2019.

CHAPTER 5. ACT UP AND THE AIDS CRISIS

1. Maria L. La Ganga. "The First Lady Who Looked Away: Nancy and the Reagans' Troubling AIDS Legacy." *Guardian*, 11 Mar. 2016, theguardian.com. Accessed 7 Jan. 2019.

2. "History of AIDS." *History*, 13 July 2017, history.com. Accessed 7 Jan. 2019.

3. "History of AIDS."

4. "HIV/AIDS." *World Health Organization*, n.d., who.int. Accessed 7 Jan. 2019.

5. "Global HIV/AIDS Overview." *HIV.gov*, n.d., hiv.gov. Accessed 7 Jan. 2019.

6. German Lopez. "The Reagan Administration's Unbelievable Response to the HIV/AIDS Epidemic." *Vox*, 1 Dec. 2016, vox.com. Accessed 7 Jan. 2019.

7. La Ganga, "The First Lady Who Looked Away."

8. Craig A. Rimmerman. "ACT UP." *Body*, n.d., thebody.com. Accessed 7 Jan. 2019.

9. "History of the Quilt." *AIDS Memorial Quilt*, n.d., aidsquilt.org. Accessed 7 Jan. 2019.

10. "AZT's Inhuman Cost." *New York Times*, 28 Aug. 1989, nytimes.com. Accessed 7 Jan. 2019.

SOURCE NOTES CONTINUED

11. "Mortality Rates Among People with HIV, Long on the Wane, Continue to Drop." *POZ*, 4 Feb. 2013, poz.com. Accessed 7 Jan. 2019.

12. David Ansen. "A Lost Generation." *Newsweek*, 17 Jan. 1993, newsweek.com. Accessed 7 Jan. 2019.

13. "HIV in the United States." *Centers for Disease Control and Prevention*, n.d., cdc.gov. Accessed 7 Jan. 2019.

14. "HIV in the United States."

CHAPTER 6. MAKING A FAMILY

1. Robin Toner. "A Gay Rights Rally Over Gains and Goals." *New York Times*, 1 May 2000, nytimes.com. Accessed 7 Jan. 2019.

2. Reginald Hardwick. "Michigan LGBTQ Pride Parade/Rally Focuses on Families & Diversity." *WKAR*, 17 June 2018, www.wkar.org. Accessed 7 Jan. 2019.

3. Isabel Dobrin. "ACLU Sues Michigan After Same-Sex Couples Seeking to Adopt Are Rejected." *NPR*, 23 Sept. 2017, npr.org. Accessed 7 Jan. 2019.

4. Zach Ford. "Family Acceptance Is the Biggest Factor for Positive LGBT Youth Outcomes, Study Finds." *Think Progress*, 24 June 2015, thinkprogress.org. Accessed 7 Jan. 2019.

5. Julie Compton. "Republican Adoption Amendment Would Hurt LGBTQ Foster Youth, Advocates Say." *NBC News*, 30 July 2018, nbcnews.com. Accessed 7 Jan. 2019.

6. "LGBT Homelessness." *National Collation for the Homeless*, n.d., nationalhomeless.org. Accessed 7 Jan. 2019.

7. "About Us." *Ali Forney Center*, n.d., aliforneycenter.org. Accessed 7 Jan. 2019.

8. "Mission & Impact." *Zebra Coalition*, n.d., zebrayouth.org. Accessed 7 Jan. 2019.

CHAPTER 7. HUMAN RIGHTS

1. "HCR's Changing Roles." *Cornell University*, n.d., rmc.library.cornell.edu. Accessed 7 Jan. 2019.

2. Trudy Ring. "HCR Defends Endorsing a Republican for Senate." *Advocate*, 24 Mar. 2016, advocate.com. Accessed 7 Jan. 2019.

3. Shabab Ahmed Mirza and Caitlin Rooney. "Discrimination Prevents LGBTQ People from Accessing Health Care." *Center for American Progress*, 18 Jan. 2018, americanprogress.org. Accessed 7 Jan. 2019.

4. Kate Kendell. "More Than Resistance: Persistence and LGBTQ Movement-Building." *San Francisco Bay Times*, n.d., sfbaytimes.com. Accessed 7 Jan. 2019.

5. Mitch Kellaway. "Meet Obama's Newest Trans Appointee: Attorney Shannon Minter." *Advocate*, 9 June 2015, advocate.com. Accessed 7 Jan. 2019.

6. Julie Compton. "Conversation Therapy or 'Identity Workshop'? Church Program Causes Uproar." *NBC News*, 26 Feb. 2018, nbcnews.com. Accessed 7 Jan. 2019.

7. Drew Howard. "Community Members to Protest 'Conversion Therapy' Workshop." *Pride Source*, 7 Feb. 2018, pridesource.com. Accessed 7 Jan. 2019.

8. "Born Perfect: Laws & Legislation by State." *NCLR*, n.d., nclrights.org. Accessed 7 Jan. 2019.

CHAPTER 8. WHO GETS TO BE LGBTQ?

1. "Nightmare: Teen Boy Harasses Girls in Their Bathroom, Colo. School Tells Girls They Have No Rights." *Pacific Justice Institute*, 10 Oct. 2013, pacificjustice.org. Accessed 7 Jan. 2019.

2. "The Report of the 2015 US Transgender Survey." *National Center for Transgender Equality*, Dec. 2016, transequality.org. Accessed 7 Jan. 2019.

3. "Statistics." *NCADV*, n.d., ncadv.org. Accessed 7 Jan. 2019.

4. "The Report of the 2015 US Transgender Survey."

5. Trudy Ring. "This Year's Michigan Womyn's Music Festival Will Be the Last." *Advocate*, 21 Apr. 2015, advocate.com. Accessed 7 Jan. 2019.

6. "Log Cabin Republicans Oppose Trump Transgender Military Statement." *Log Cabin Republicans*, 26 July 2017, logcabin.org. Accessed 7 Jan. 2019.

7. "About Us." *Log Cabin Republicans*, n.d., logcabin.org. Accessed 7 Jan. 2019.

8. Kasandra Brabaw. "Why We Call Ourselves Queers, Dykes, Fags, & Homos." *Refinery29*, 15 Nov. 2017, refinery29.com. Accessed 7 Jan. 2019.

9. "Forums." *Asexual Visibility & Education Network*, n.d., asexuality.org. Accessed 7 Jan. 2019.

CHAPTER 9. THE FUTURE OF SOCIAL MOVEMENTS

1. Sima Shakeri. "Television Has a 'Bury Your Gays,' Queerbaiting, and LGBTQ Representation Problem." *Huffpost*, 30 June 2017, huffingtonpost.ca. Accessed 7 Jan. 2019.

2. Shakeri, "Television Has a 'Bury Your Gays,' Queerbaiting, and LGBTQ Representation Problem."

3. Shakeri, "Television Has a 'Bury Your Gays,' Queerbaiting, and LGBTQ Representation Problem."

4. Marie Lyn Bernard. "All 202 Dead Lesbian and Bisexual Characters on TV, and How They Died." *Autostraddle*, 11 Mar. 2016, autostraddle.com. Accessed 7 Jan. 2019.

5. Angela Watercutter. "It's Harder to Kill Off Gay Characters When They're Trending." *Wired*, 14 Apr. 2016, wired.com. Accessed 7 Jan. 2019.

6. Kimberlé Crenshaw. "Demarginalizing the Intersection of Race and Sex." *University of Chicago*, n.d., chicagounbound.uchicago.edu. Accessed 7 Jan. 2019.

7. Kristin Moe. "The Evolution of 'Intersectionality:' From a Theory to a Way to Fight Back." *AlterNet*, 9 Apr. 2014, alternet.org. Accessed 7 Jan. 2019.

8. Gabriel Arana. "White Gay Men Are Hindering Our Progress as a Queer Community." *Them*, 9 Nov. 2017, them.us. Accessed 7 Jan. 2019.

9. Gracie Awalt. "Banned Blood Drive Protests FDA Regulations." *Daily Texan*, 1 Mar. 2018, dailytexanonline.com. Accessed 7 Jan. 2019.

10. Romy Oltuski. "Laverne Cox Sounds Off about Trump's Transgender Military Ban." *InStyle*, 26 Jul. 2017, instyle.com. Accessed 25 Jan. 2019.

11. Umber Ghauri. "Queer, Disabled People Like Me Are Excluded from LGBTQ+ Spaces—It Is Dividing Our Community." *Independent*, 15 Feb. 2018, independent.co.uk. Accessed 7 Jan. 2019.

12. Leslie Feinberg. *Trans Liberation: Beyond Pink or Blue*. Boston, MA: Beacon, 1998. 107.

INDEX

ABOUT THE AUTHORS

DUCHESS HARRIS, JD, PHD

Dr. Harris is a professor of American Studies at Macalester College and curator of the Duchess Harris Collection of ABDO books. She is also the coauthor of the titles in the collection, which features popular selections such as *Hidden Human Computers: The Black Women of NASA* and series including News Literacy and Being Female in America.

Before working with ABDO, Dr. Harris authored several other books on the topics of race, culture, and American history. She served as an associate editor for *Litigation News*, the American Bar Association Section of Litigation's quarterly flagship publication, and was the first editor in chief of *Law Raza*, an interactive online journal covering race and the law, published at William Mitchell College of Law. She has earned a PhD in American Studies from the University of Minnesota and a JD from William Mitchell College of Law.

MARTHA LUNDIN

Martha Lundin graduated with a Master of Fine Arts in Creative Writing from the University of North Carolina Wilmington in 2017. They now live and work in Minnesota.